50 Creative Training Openers & Energizers

Innovative Ways to Start Your Training with a BANG!

Bob Pike, CSP, CPAE

Lynn Solem

JOSSEY-BASS/PFEIFFER
A Wiley Company
www.pfeiffer.com

Published by

JOSSEY-BASS/PFEIFFER

A Wiley Company
989 Market Street
San Francisco, CA 94103-1741
415.433.1740; Fax 415.433.0499
800.274.4434; Fax 800.569.0443

www.pfeiffer.com

7620 West 78th Street
Minneapolis, MN 55439
(800) 383-9210
(612) 829-1954; Fax (612) 829-0260

Visit our website at:
http://www.creativetrainingtech.com

Jossey-Bass/Pfeiffer is a registered trademark of John Wiley & Sons, Inc.

ISBN: 0-7879-5303-2
Library of Congress Catalog Card Number 99-054008

Library of Congress Cataloging-in-Publication Data
Pike, Robert W.
  50 creative training openers and energizers: innovative ways to start your training
with a bang!/Bob Pike, Lynn Solem.
      p. cm.
   ISBN 0-7879-5303-2 (alk. paper)
    1. Training. 2. Activity programs in education. 3. Group games. I. Title: Fifty
creative training openers and energizers. II. Solem, Lynn. III. Title.
LB1027.47 .P53 2000
331.25'92—dc21   99-054008

Acquiring Editor: Matthew Holt
Director of Development: Kathleen Dolan Davies
Developmental Editor: Rebecca Taff
Senior Production Editor: Dawn Kilgore
Manufacturing Supervisor: Becky Carreño

Printed in the United States of America

Printing 10   9   8   7   6   5   4   3

Contents

☑ Icebreaker

☑ Networker

☑ Team Builder

☑ Task Tension

☑ Relationship Tension

☑ Personal Tension

☑ Focus Activity

*Bonus openers

Openers Matrix

☑ Icebreaker
☑ Networker
☑ Team Builder
☑ Task Tension
☑ Relationship Tension
☑ Personal Tension
☑ Focus Activity

	Icebreaker	Networker	Team Builder	Task Tension	Relationship Tension	Personal Tension	Focus Activity
Autobiography	✓	✓			✓		✓
Banana Split	✓				✓	✓	✓
Business Card Introduction	✓	✓			✓		✓
Choose Five	✓				✓	✓	✓
Coins	✓				✓		✓
Customized License Plates	✓		✓		✓		✓
Double Circles	✓	✓			✓		
Dream and Nightmares	✓		✓	✓	✓		✓
Excess Baggage	✓		✓	✓	✓	✓	✓
Eye Opener				✓			✓
Five People	✓		✓		✓		✓
Five Traits	✓				✓	✓	✓
Four C's	✓				✓		✓
Four-Quadrant Name Tent	✓				✓		✓
Gift Opener	✓		✓	✓	✓		✓
Group Milling	✓	✓			✓		✓
Hail to the Chief	✓		✓		✓		✓

	Icebreaker	Networker	Team Builder	Task Tension	Relationship Tension	Personal Tension	Focus Activity
Hands Full	✓		✓	✓	✓		✓
Human Scavenger Hunt	✓	✓			✓		✓
Interview the Trainer	✓			✓	✓		✓
The "Intro" You Deserve	✓				✓		✓
Key Questions			✓		✓		✓
Let's Get Acquainted	✓	✓			✓		✓
Let's Share	✓				✓		✓
Lifeline	✓				✓		✓
M & M®s	✓		✓	✓	✓		✓
Metaphor Opener	✓		✓	✓	✓		✓
Musical Teams	✓	✓			✓		✓
My Hopes	✓				✓		✓
My Life As a TV Show	✓			✓	✓		✓
Name Tent Anchor	✓			✓	✓		✓
Name Tent for Class "Ownership"	✓		✓	✓	✓		✓
Name Tent Interview	✓	✓			✓		✓
Name Tent Spoof	✓		✓		✓		✓
Name Tent Visual	✓				✓		✓
Nicknames	✓				✓		✓
Other Half Interview	✓	✓			✓	✓	✓
Personalized Coat of Arms	✓				✓		✓
Playing Card Introduction	✓	✓			✓		✓
Ragged Start	✓		✓	✓	✓		✓
Random Numbers	✓				✓		✓
Silly Hats	✓			✓	✓		✓
Silly Sentences	✓		✓	✓	✓		✓
Six "H" Name Tent	✓				✓		✓
Striptease	✓				✓		✓

	Icebreaker	Networker	Team Builder	Task Tension	Relationship Tension	Personal Tension	Focus Activity
Things You Carry	✓				✓		✓
To Be a Success	✓		✓	✓	✓		✓
"Tomorrow I'm Going to...."	✓			✓	✓		✓
Toothpick Confessions	✓		✓		✓		✓
Twenty Questions	✓	✓			✓		✓
Two, Three, and Four Things	✓				✓		✓
Uniqueness and Commonalities	✓		✓		✓		✓
Unusual Props	✓		✓	✓	✓		✓
Unusual Request	✓			✓			✓
Vote Your Priorities			✓	✓	✓		✓
What Can You Do with It?			✓	✓	✓		✓
What Would Your Best Friend Say?	✓				✓	✓	✓
What's Your Line?	✓				✓		✓
What's Your Role?	✓			✓	✓		✓
Worst Day Ever	✓		✓	✓	✓		✓
Write a Commercial	✓				✓		✓

Introduction

- ☑ Icebreaker
- ☑ Networker
- ☑ Team Builder
- ☑ Task Tension
- ☑ Relationship Tension
- ☑ Personal Tension
- ☑ Focus Activity

Why We Use Openers and Energizers

Our participants come into the classroom with their brains "full." They are distracted, probably on overload from their work duties. The training may be a job interruption; they often are not even sure what the class content may be. If we start to deliver content without breaking through the learners' mental, and possibly emotional, state, both their motivation to learn and their retention of what is learned will be sadly lacking. If they don't retain it, how can they use it?

In Creative Training Techniques™ we focus on the six components of memory and on how the brain works. Openers are important because one of those aspects of memory is *"primacy,"* the tendency to remember the *beginning* of a list, presentation, sequence, or training experience. Thus, how we open sets the tone for the rest of the class and is vital in gaining attention, breaking preoccupation, and establishing a learning atmosphere.

Portmanteau: adj. Combining more than one use or quality.

—Merriam Webster Collegiate Dictionary

Different Types of Openers

The word "opener" for a trainer is a portmanteau word, for openers can be used for a combination of uses. Openers generally serve from one to three functions in a training or teaching classroom: (1) they can serve to build a team, in that those participating tend to bond through the completion of a task; (2) they can be good for networking, helping participants build a web of resources while becoming acquainted; and (3) they can be icebreakers, as all training settings need some activity that focuses the learner in the classroom.

As you read through the sixty-one openers offered in this book, think about the setting in which you will be training. You'll know whether a team builder, a networker, or an icebreaker would be most effective for your purposes. Many openers, being portmanteau in nature, can be used for more than one purpose at once.

Networkers and team builders may be called for later in your training session, in which case use appropriate activities from this book freely. In fact, you may find it appropriate to use more than one. For example, you can use exercises identified for team building in a class setting if your content lends itself to team building, quality circles, job sharing, and so on. If you train using teams and switch teams as you move through the day, some of the openers presented here will be needed at each switch.

The Role of Tension in the Classroom

In addition to the different purposes discussed above, openers also serve to reduce tension, which inhibits retention also. The right opener can serve to reduce tension in your classrooms. Participants may come into the classroom with any one of several types of tension: *task, relationship,* and/or *personal.*

Task tension would apply when we ask a learner to tackle a completely new task, format, or learning experience. An example would be learning new software or, for new employees, grasping rules, regulations, and policies. *Relationship tension* can come into play if learners have been previously embarrassed in the classroom or fear that they will be asked to do something embarrassing in front of others. They basically feel tense about being singled out in the classroom setting.

Personal tension can, of course, range from concern about a project that's been left behind or an expected phone call to the very real and serious challenges that may be going on in a learner's life.

The right opener can reassure learners as to their ability to learn the material or task; make learners comfortable in the safety of the learning setting; and distract learners from many personal challenges by focusing their attention on the classroom. (More than one beginning activity may be needed when learners have a lot of tension.) As you scan through the openers you will be able to find activities that help your learners reduce their tension.

In a recent class we asked thirty-five participants to network and to share what they thought were the best ways to reduce tension. Some of the things that participants said were: "Create a safe environment," "Allow them to vent," and "Begin with an opener." We could picture a novice trainer asking an experienced trainer for advice and hearing those three responses. Although they are "correct," that novice might walk away shaking his or her head, for those are ideas for "what to do" and not for "how to do."

A quick example of an "allow them to vent" activity might be to give each person an envelope and a 3" x 5" card. The envelope can be called a "worry envelope" or a "distraction envelope." Have the participants write on the card all the things they have to do or are concerned about that could get in the way of the learning. You might have them share two things they wrote down, which would be an ice-breaker (but that step is optional). Then ask them to set the envelopes aside and not open them again until the end of class. Just that simple activity can do much to clear the learners' minds and "venting" takes place.

Another venting exercise that is particularly effective when there is organizational flux and change, and in those cases in which there might be organizational disgruntlement, involves the use of team charts. You will want to hang clean flip-chart sheets up in the training room before class, one for each team. You might begin by asking, "Have you ever been in a training class in which those attending had issues to discuss, real and valid issues, but issues that had nothing to do with the class content?" You will see heads nodding in agreement. Then you might say, "Let's surface similar issues for this class and get them out of the way. Please go with your team members to the wall and find a blank sheet. Take your markers and build a list of. . . ." Here you will want to put in your own title. Recommendations include: "Things We Can't Do Anything About in This Room," "Distractions Chart," or "Issues Chart."

A variation of this might be to give team members Post-it® pads and have them list, one issue per Post-it, what is on their minds. Then adhere the Post-it Notes to the sheets. (*An Aside:* Post-it Notes won't stick to the 3M self-sticking charts.)

A simple way to ease relationship tensions, and to help your learners feel safe, is just to announce that they are in a safe environment. It may seem obvious to you, but it might not be obvious to them, and the announcement helps.

In this book we will give you many more "how-to-do" activities. They will help you create a safe environment, allow learners to vent and release tension, and find the exact opener you need.

Time Allocated for Openers

Even a one-hour class will benefit from an icebreaker, for all of the reasons mentioned above, but primarily to focus attention in the classroom, to break through the participants' preoccupation, when they're with you physically, but are not with you mentally. They may be looking right at you while thinking of projects they have to do, calls that have to be returned, messages that need to be written, or any one of a hundred other things.

For a one-hour class, you might want to devote five minutes to your opener. What would that be like? With crossword puzzle software and teams, a great five-minute opener might be to use the software and take ten minutes to create a ten-clue crossword based on your content. Then have a copy of the crossword at each place. Have an overhead displayed that asks learners to take the first three minutes of class and work with others to complete the crossword.

This is not only an icebreaker and focus exercise, but it achieves three other worthy goals: (1) It is a team builder, for it involves the completion of a task; (2) it introduces content and alerts learners to what's important; and (3) it lets you know, during the two-minute debriefing, what the knowledge level of the class might be. (This activity is repeated in the exercise portion of this book.)

A three- or four-hour class would call for a ten-minute opener. A full day, a twenty-minute opener, and if there is a switch of teams at the lunch break, you will want a ten-minute opener for the second half. If you are training over multiple days, you might want a twenty-minute opener on Day 1 and a ten-minute opener on each succeeding day.

Group Introductions

So often trainers automatically begin classes by having the participants stand up, one by one, and introduce themselves. This may not be inappropriate in a class of eight or fewer people, although there might be better ways, as learners go through four "levels of socialization" at the beginning of a training session.

The first stage people are in as they enter the training room is that of being alone—the sense of *isolation*. An easy and effective way for the trainer to break through this stage is to greet each person as he or she enters the room. A welcome and a handshake offer trainees the opportunity to "bond" with one other person (the trainer) and break through the sense of isolation.

The second level of socialization is to form a diad. Even strangers will be fairly comfortable talking to one other person. For that reason many trainers prepare an "interview sheet," pair off the trainees (if there is an odd number the trainer becomes one of the participants), and has each member of the pair interview the other. Questions can include experience in the content, length of time with the organization, and a variety of nonthreatening but directed questions. Then as each person introduces his or her partner to the group, the networking has begun, the partners become "teams," and yet individuals are not feeling a great deal of nervousness.

The third level of socialization is the formation of teams of up to six people. People will share with ease in a small, safe group when they would be quite uncomfortable speaking in front of nine or more people. This is especially true when the group has a task to complete.

The fourth level of socialization is speaking in front of a large group. Many studies have placed the fear of public speaking in people's top ten fears, ranking right up there with death by several different means. For this reason, we discourage trainers from beginning a class of twelve or more people by asking individuals to stand up and introduce themselves. In Creative Training Techniques™ the first information that is shared is the group leader report, wherein—following a powerful opening—an individual tells what was discussed at the table, a much different and less threatening task than talking about oneself.

Room Setup

An inviting training room can begin to dissipate tension before the class begins. Try to arrange your room so that teams can be formed easily. Round tables or chairs set in rectangles with the appropriate number of chairs invite participants to begin the team-building process.

It is a good idea to have several colorful charts already on the walls so that information is available before class starts. They also create a welcoming atmosphere.

It is helpful to have a pre-class activity, such as "work on the crossword with others" or "solve this quiz with others." This starts the networking and group process. It gives early arrivals something to do and helps to transition into the subject matter through a debriefing of content-based activities.

Risk Levels

There are high-risk, medium-risk, and low-risk ways to open your classes. You will want to fit the risk level of the activity to the level of those in the class. An example of a low-risk opener would be to have participants fill out a simple question sheet and share their answers with their team members, as opposed to sharing personal information with everyone in the room. Such things as names of pets, states of birth, length of time with the organization, favorite cartoon characters, and so on are low-risk questions.

A medium-risk opener would be the "interview your partner and share what he or she said with everyone in the room" exercise discussed earlier.

A high-risk opener would be to stand in front of the whole room and "tell about yourself." Another example of a high-risk opener would be "share an embarrassing moment."

The Use of Teams

In Creative Training Techniques™ we stress the use of teams. One wonderful benefit of doing so is the reduction of tension. Just having a learning partner reduces tension—creating an "I'm not here alone" feeling. But forming teams can also produce tension. Thought needs to be taken as to when groups should be re-formed. Many trainers begin their classes by counting off and reseating people immediately. The up side of that approach is that the deadly duo, terrible trio, and quarrelsome quartets have been broken up. If the people you train work together and have formed cliques that are likely to disrupt the class, you might want to form new teams immediately.

When participants do not know one another well, the immediate formation of new teams can create unnecessary tension, particularly if strangers came into the room and began to work on a pre-class activity. In this case you might wait until the lunch break to form new teams.

The method you use to form teams can also create tension. Creative Training Techniques Senior Trainer, Lori Backer, gives examples of high-risk, medium-risk, and low-risk team formation activities:

> "Low-risk team formation can be to use color-coded paper clips, flags, or markers, and have all like colors find each other. Medium risk could be to draw a picture of one's birth month. Have everyone stand up and, without speaking, form a line in order of the twelve months, identifying position by drawing only. When all are in line, you can count off by pairs, triads, or other number to form teams. An example of a high-risk team formation process would be to distribute cards with either animal names or physical gestures (such as winking, high fiving, laughing, jumping, etc.). For a class of twenty people, if you want five to a team, you would make five identical cards, four sets of cards. Individuals would have to 'find' their teammates by either making the animal sound or by doing the physical gesture without speaking. Participants mill until teams of five are formed."

A second powerful benefit of working in small groups is the opportunity presented for the knowledge in the room to surface and be shared. When we train people in a classroom style seating, eye contact is exclusively with the trainer, and all too often the request to ask a question or share an idea is not acted on. By having our learners in small groups, assignments can be given, such as, "Take ninety seconds and, as a team, come up with two questions you'd like to have answered" or "Take ninety seconds and, as a team, come up with the three ideas you've found most valuable so far."

Teams can also serve to dissipate any hostility from experienced learners. The trainer can ask everyone to stand and then say, "If you have a year or less of experience (in this topic) or (with this organization) please be seated. . . . Three or fewer years, please be seated. . . ." This is continued until an appropriate number of "experienced" people are still standing. The trainer can then ask those who are standing to be part of an advisory panel, willing to help answer questions and to offer ideas. The experienced learners form a team, and although they may not sit together, they play a special role and usually feel good about having their experience acknowledged and honored.

Attention Getters

There are times when we only have twenty minutes to spend with a group. In those settings we need quick attention getters; Creative Training Techniques Trainer Sue Ensz calls these "sixty second openers."

Bob Pike, in his book *High Impact Presentations,* suggests quick openers like these:

✓ One approach is to outline an incident or tell a story. Stories capture attention and are particularly effective if they involve the company, the job, the family, or the trainer's own experience.

✓ A second approach is to ask for a show of hands. A participant who has raised his or her hand is "present" in the room in more than one sense of the word. The question can be job-related or life-related. It might be effective if phrased, "Have you ever experienced . . . ?"

✓ Another approach is to ask a question, which is particularly effective if asked of a team. A question asked early in Creative Training Techniques is, "What was the value of the brain teaser? Take ninety seconds to decide, as a team, what the values were." This question refers to the pre-class activity they experienced. Asking a question of a specific team helps you avoid asking a question to the room in general and having it be met with complete silence.

✓ Another way to capture the group's attention is by making a promise, such as, "I promise you that before this class is over, you. . . ." You can fill in the blank with what is appropriate to your content, for example:

Will be certified to . . .

Will know six ways to handle a difficult customer

Will have twenty new ideas

✓ Whatever you do, promise participants value for their time and interest. It's best to promise less than you know you will deliver and to make a formal issue of keeping the promise. Do consistent checks to make sure that the group sees that you are honoring your commitment.

✓ Laughter is a wonderful attention getter. Fun posters and pictures can help, but the old "begin with a joke" is not usually an appropriate use of humor. Self-depreciating, humorous stories can be the most effective form of humor.

✓ The use of an unusual visual aid or prop can also capture attention very quickly.

Sixty-one different openers and energizers are offered on the following pages. They serve myriad purposes, but among them you will find ice-breakers, networkers, and team builders, as well as tension reducers, ways to let your learners vent, and ways to help them feel safe.

Autobiography

- ☑ Icebreaker
- ☑ Networker
- ☐ Team Builder
- ☐ Task Tension
- ☑ Relationship Tension
- ☐ Personal Tension
- ☑ Focus Activity

Objectives Break the ice
Allow opportunities to network
Become better acquainted
Provide focus on the topic

Class Length One-half day or longer

Audience Any

Group Size Twelve or more

Time 15 to 25 minutes

Equipment One autobiography page per person (given to participants to be completed prior to class)
One master autobiography list for each participant (completed during class)
Pens or pencils for each participant

Process *NOTE:* This is a good networking exercise. It energizes the class by having people on their feet introducing themselves to one another.

Before the class, the trainer contacts the participants and asks them to fill out "autobiographies." (It is assumed that no one would mind sharing these items with the class, both personal and professional.) The autobiographies are to be returned to the trainer prior to the first class. The trainer makes a "master" autobiography list using two or three items from each person's autobiography and hands copies to participants as they arrive.

Participants are asked to begin circulating in the room to find out which items match with other participants. They are to introduce themselves and ask others to sign the sheets beside the matching items.

Autobiography

Instructions: Fill out the form below and return it to the trainer prior to class.

Name: _____

Favorite Movie: _____

Favorite Food: _____

Favorite Dessert: _____

Favorite Book: _____

Favorite Vacation Spot: _____

Favorite Song: _____

Favorite Hobby: _____

Size of High School Class: _____

Favorite Job: _____

Population of Hometown: _____

Greatest Job Strength: _____

Number of Siblings: _____

Number of Years with Present Company: _____

Age of Oldest Relative (Who?): _____

Internet Service Provider: _____

Number of Children (Boys/Girls): _____

Place of Birth: _____

Number and Type of Pets: _____

Favorite Color: _____

Master Autobiography

Instructions: Mill around the room, introduce yourself, and obtain the signatures of people who match the autobiographical detail on each of the lines below (maximum of three signatures from any one person, but several people may sign one line).

Favorite Movie: _____

Favorite Dessert: _____

Favorite Vacation Spot: _____

Favorite Hobby: _____

Favorite Job: _____

Greatest Job Strength: _____

Number of Years with Present Company: _____

Internet Service Provider: _____

Place of Birth: _____

Favorite Color: _____

Favorite Food: _____

Favorite Book: _____

Favorite Song: _____

Size of High School Class: _____

Population of Hometown: _____

Number of Siblings: _____

Age of Oldest Relative (Who?): _____

Number of Children (Boys/Girls): _____

Number and Type of Pets: _____

Banana Split

☑	Icebreaker
☐	Networker
☐	Team Builder
☐	Task Tension
☑	Relationship Tension
☑	Personal Tension
☑	Focus Activity

Objectives   Break the ice
Become better acquainted
Alleviate personal tension
Provide focus on the topic

Class Length   Ninety minutes or longer

Audience   Any

Group Size   Any number, in subgroups of three to five

Time   3 to 5 minutes

Equipment   *Optional:* A transparency or flip-chart sheet showing a banana split
Paper and pencils for each participant

Process   *NOTE:* This is a fun little icebreaker for groups or teams of three to five people. Any complex food dish can be used, such as lasagna or pizza.

The trainer breaks the group into smaller groups of three to five people, hands out pencils and paper, and asks each person to write down the part of a banana split he or she would most like to be and why. Responses are shared among the members of the small groups, or the large group if there is time or the group is small.

Business Card Introduction

☑ Icebreaker
☑ Networker
☐ Team Builder
☐ Task Tension
☑ Relationship Tension
☐ Personal Tension
☑ Focus Activity

Objectives   Break the ice
Allow opportunities to network
Become better acquainted
Provide focus on the topic

Class Length   Two hours or longer

Audience   Any

Group Size   Any number, in subgroups of six

Time   5 minutes

Equipment   Participants' business cards, if they are available, or index cards and pens for participants to make their own business cards

Process   *NOTE:* This exercise combines creativity with information sharing. Participants may use their own business cards, and/or the trainer should have index cards and pens available so that those who have not brought business cards can make their own.

Once everyone has gathered, the trainer asks them to create a two-sided business card. One side of the card is to be used to list factual information such as name, title, organization, job function, and so forth. The other side is to be whimsical or lighter in tone, listing such things as favorite color, strongest good point, dream vacation, or other personal items. The trainer should make a card at the same time. The trainer should first share his or her own card, then have the members of the subgroups share their cards with one another (or with everyone in the room in a smaller group).

Choose Five

☑	Icebreaker
☐	Networker
☐	Team Builder
☐	Task Tension
☑	Relationship Tension
☑	Personal Tension
☑	Focus Activity

Objectives
Break the ice
Become better acquainted
Alleviate personal tension
Provide focus on the topic

Class Length
Two hours or longer

Audience
Any

Group Size
Any number, in subgroups of five to seven

Time
5 to 10 minutes

Equipment
One sheet of open-ended sentences per person
Enough pencils for all participants

Process
The trainer hands out the sheet of open-ended sentences and pencils and asks participants to select and complete any five of the sentence stems.
Participants then share in small groups why they selected particular stems and how they completed them.

Options
Some of the sentence stems are job-oriented and some are personal.

The trainer can add, delete, or change any of them to shift the focus of discussion.

The trainer can allow groups to complete and share additional phrases periodically during the day as an energizer.

Choose Five Sentence Completions

Instructions: Choose five of the following sentence stems and complete them. You will then share your responses within your group.

1. The department I work in is....

2. My three all-time favorite movies are....

3. In high school, I was considered....

4. Outside of work, I am good at....

5. My favorite food is....

6. My favorite fiction book is....

7. My favorite nonfiction book is....

8. The best part of my job is....

9. The worst part of my job is....

10. My favorite TV show is/was....

11. The best vacation I ever took was....

12. If I could change one thing about myself it would be....

13. What I like best about myself is....

14. A perfect party would include....

15. The greatest strength I bring to this class is....

Coins

☑	Icebreaker
☐	Networker
☐	Team Builder
☐	Task Tension
☑	Relationship Tension
☐	Personal Tension
☑	Focus Activity

Objectives Break the ice
Become better acquainted
Provide focus on the topic

Class Length Ninety minutes or longer

Audience Any

Group Size Any number, in subgroups of five to seven

Time 5 to 10 minutes

Equipment One to fifteen extra coins in case people can't borrow enough to make a total of six coins per person

Process Participants should be divided into small teams (ideally five to seven per team).

The trainer asks each participant to find or borrow six coins of any denomination.

After each person has six coins, the trainer asks them to look at the years the coins were minted and then to choose three or four of the coins and recall one significant (and positive) thing that happened to them during each of those years.

Once everyone has recalled their significant events, the trainer asks everyone to take turns sharing their information with members of their subgroups.

NOTE: The reason that participants are asked to select more coins than events to be shared is that someone may have a coin minted in a year in which a traumatic event happened. By having more coins, the person may skip that year and move to a memory of a happier event.

Customized License Plates

☑ Icebreaker
☐ Networker
☑ Team Builder
☐ Task Tension
☑ Relationship Tension
☐ Personal Tension
☑ Focus Activity

Objectives Break the ice
Allow opportunities to build teams
Become better acquainted
Provide focus on the topic

Class Length Three hours or longer

Audience Any

Group Size Any number, in subgroups of five to seven

Time 10 to 15 minutes

Equipment One sheet of sample license plates with answers for the trainer
Enough copies of the blank license plate template and pencils for all participants

Process *NOTE:* This activity can be done either by individuals or by teams. Business cards can also be designed, rather than license plates.

The trainer reminds participants of the limited space available on a license plate (or business card) for sending a message. He or she can display the sample license plates if desired.

Every participant then receives a blank license plate and a pencil, and the trainer asks everyone to create a personal message to share using only six to eight letters or numbers.

If this activity is being done in teams, the trainer emphasizes that all participants should contribute to the effort.

License plate messages can convey a desired goal, a value held, a favorite saying, a learning point from the course (if used later in the course), or something personal for sharing either in small groups or with the entire class.

GR8ONE
Great one (You or Wayne Gretsky)

SOSUME
So Sue Me

BITERITE
Bite Right (your dentist)

TOPMGR
Top Manager (your goal?)

MTFBWY
May the Force Be with You (for Star Wars fans)

HRLYRDR
Harley (Davidson motorcycle) Rider

Sample Customized License Plates

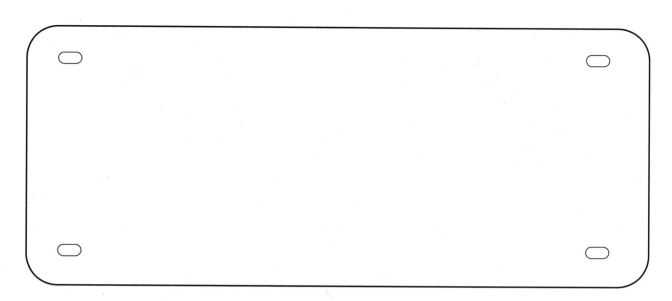

Customized License Plate Template

Double Circles

- ☑ Icebreaker
- ☑ Networker
- ☐ Team Builder
- ☐ Task Tension
- ☑ Relationship Tension
- ☐ Personal Tension
- ☐ Focus Activity

Objectives Break the ice
Allow opportunities to network
Become better acquainted

Class Length One-half day or longer

Audience Any

Group Size At least ten, but no more than twenty-four

Time 15 to 20 minutes

Equipment One 3" x 5" index card per person for taking notes
A pencil for each person

Process *NOTE:* This is an effective way to divide participants into small groups and at the same time gauge the experience levels that exist in the group.

The trainer divides the participants into two groups and has Group 1 form a circle facing inward and Group 2 form a circle inside the first, facing outward so that each person looks at a partner.

The trainer tells the outer group to move clockwise and the inner group to move counterclockwise, stopping as they meet each new person.

Each time that the group moves, each person is to introduce himself or herself by stating name and one other fact (to be determined by the trainer, such as how long on the job, which department, or what organization).

After a few moments, the trainer asks the inner circle to stand still, but the outer group continues moving clockwise until the trainer says, "Stop."

At that point, the trainer has the people directly facing one another spend a few minutes talking about the expertise they bring to the class. Partners then introduce each other to the whole group, including the experience the other person has.

The trainer can form small groups based on experience if desired.

Dreams and Nightmares

☑ Icebreaker

☐ Networker

☑ Team Builder

☑ Task Tension

☑ Relationship Tension

☐ Personal Tension

☑ Focus Activity

Objectives Break the ice
Allow opportunities to build teams
Relieve tension associated with a topic
Become better acquainted
Provide focus on the topic

Class Length Two hours or longer

Audience Any

Group Size Up to seventy, in subgroups of five to seven

Time 5 to 8 minutes

Equipment Two 3" x 5" index cards per participant (preferably two different colors)
A transparency of the sample card template

Process *NOTE:* This activity is best when preceded by a team opener, so that individuals feel safe and part of a team before beginning. The exercise is humorous, stimulates conversations, and helps participants realize they are not alone in their feelings.

The trainer gives every participant two index cards and asks them to label the card of one color "dreams" and the card of the other color "nightmares." He or she tells people *not* to put their names on the cards.

The trainer then asks everyone to list their positive feelings about coming to the training session on the dream card and their negative feelings on the nightmare card.

Everyone then shares their dreams and nightmares within their own teams.

The trainer collects the cards, sorts them into dreams and nightmares, and then posts what everyone has written for the participants to read during breaks.

Options The trainer can give participants three to five small adhesive-backed dots to place on the dreams or nightmares they share after they have been posted.

Teams can suggest ground rules or guidelines for the class that would help the dreams come true and banish the nightmares.

Periodically, the trainer can give people a chance to revisit the cards. As the dreams come true, the trainer can have participants mark that card in a special way, perhaps with stars or a colored border. As the nightmares are banished, the participant who wrote it can put a big "X" through the card with a marker.

Sample Dreams and Nightmares Cards

BONUS!

Excess Baggage

☑ Icebreaker
☐ Networker
☑ Team Builder
☑ Task Tension
☑ Relationship Tension
☑ Personal Tension
☑ Focus Activity

Objectives   Break the ice
Allow opportunities to build teams
Relieve tension associated with a topic
Become better acquainted
Alleviate personal tension
Provide focus on the topic

Class Length   One hour or longer

Audience   Any

Group Size   Any number

Time   5 to 8 minutes

Equipment   A supply of 3" x 5" index cards for every participant
A small, empty suitcase

Process   The trainer asks participants to brainstorm all the reasons why the class may not be a good and/or useful experience for them and to write each reason on a separate card.

The trainer then opens the suitcase and asks participants to "unload the baggage" that might keep them from benefiting from the class.

Participants can write ways to overcome their potential "baggage" and share their ideas in small groups, tossing the cards into the suitcase for dramatic effect.

Eye Opener

☐ Icebreaker
☐ Networker
☐ Team Builder
☑ Task Tension
☐ Relationship Tension
☐ Personal Tension
☑ Focus Activity

Objectives   Relieve tension associated with a topic
Provide focus on the topic

Class Length   Two hours or longer

Audience   Any

Group Size   Up to one hundred and fifty

Time   5 to 10 minutes

Equipment   Six to eight prepared wall charts
A prepared transparency of the questions
Paper and pencils for participants
A number of large, round, colored file folder labels or Post-it® Notes
(if using the Options)

Process   *NOTE:* The trainer might wish to precede this activity with an icebreaker. The activity requires that participants pay close attention and be aware of information posted on charts, but can reduce tension by giving participants a task to do.

The trainer places six to eight flip-chart sheets on the walls containing sayings, quotes, statistics, or whatever is desired, relating to the participants and the course content.

The trainer then posts a list of questions, such as the following, and asks participants to answer as many as possible. A great many possibilities exist for questions about subject matter.

1. Find one statement that intrigues you.

2. Find one item you agree with.

3. Find one thing that you might question.

4. Find one new and valuable piece of information.

Participants list their answers on their papers and then share their choices within their teams.

Options The trainer can prepare charts with headings on them but with no data. Some headings might include:

Things we can't do anything about in this room.

Things that are distractions inside this room.

Things that are distractions outside this room.

Things that could make this class successful.

The trainer could give each person a Post-it® Note pad and ask them to visit the various charts and add any ideas that come to mind, one per note. When everyone has finished, the trainer can ask people to vote for their key points by placing dots next to their choices.
Then the trainer could conclude with a discussion of how to deal with the issues to build a powerful course together.

Five People

☑	Icebreaker
☐	Networker
☑	Team Builder
☐	Task Tension
☑	Relationship Tension
☐	Personal Tension
☑	Focus Activity

Objectives   Break the ice
Allow opportunities to build teams
Become better acquainted
Provide focus on the topic

Class Length   Three hours or longer

Audience   Any

Group Size   Any group of twelve or more, in subgroups of five to seven

Time   10 to 15 minutes

Equipment   One 3" x 5" index card for each participant
A pencil or pen for each participant
A flip chart and felt-tipped markers

Process   As participants arrive, the trainer gives them each a 3" x 5" index card and a pen or pencil and asks them to write down the answers to the following question, posted on the flip chart:

"If you could bring five people, alive or dead, real or fictional, into a room for a discussion, who would you bring and what would you have them discuss?"

When the class starts, the trainer asks participants to share their answers within their small groups or with the large group if there is time.

Next, the trainer asks the small groups to reach consensus on a "team" answer for the questions.

BONUS!

Five Traits

☑	Icebreaker
☐	Networker
☐	Team Builder
☐	Task Tension
☑	Relationship Tension
☑	Personal Tension
☑	Focus Activity

Objectives   Break the ice
Become better acquainted
Alleviate personal tension
Provide focus on the topic

Class Length   Three hours or longer

Audience   Any

Group Size   Any group of twelve or more, in subgroups of five to seven

Time   10 to 12 minutes

Equipment   One name tent per person
One copy per person of the traits template, cut into separate traits by the trainer
Several staplers or tape dispensers placed in convenient locations

Process   The trainer must know, in advance, how many participants will be in the class. The trainer copies and cuts up as many traits sheets as there are participants and places the words in individual piles. There must be enough slips with each word so that each participant could have one of the words if so desired.

As the participants arrive, the trainer hands out name tents and asks everyone to look over all the piles and choose at least five words that they feel are descriptive of their own traits.

The trainer tells participants to staple or tape the traits they have chosen to their name tents and then share with their teams (or the group, if it is small enough) why they chose those particular words.

Enthusiastic	Cautious	Good Natured	Friendly
Accurate	Outspoken	Conventional	Decisive
Adventurous	Insightful	Persuasive	Observant
Tactful	Brave	Inspiring	Cheerful
Stimulating	Kind	Perceptive	Independent
Competitive	Logical	Loyal	Charming
Sociable	Patient	Self-Reliant	Thorough
Confident	Well-Disciplined	Persistent	Good Mixer
Contented	Cooperative	Direct	Even Tempered
Neighborly	Careful	Respectful	Optimistic

Five Traits Template

Four C's

- ☑ Icebreaker
- ☐ Networker
- ☐ Team Builder
- ☐ Task Tension
- ☑ Relationship Tension
- ☐ Personal Tension
- ☑ Focus Activity

Objectives   Break the ice
Become better acquainted
Provide focus on the topic

Class Length   One-half day or longer

Audience   Any

Group Size   Any number, in subgroups of five to seven

Time   15 minutes

Equipment   Copies of the Four C's Template for everyone, copied on index stock
A sample card on a transparency or flip-chart sheet, filled in by the trainer
Paper and a pencil for every participant

Process   The trainer asks participants to imagine that they have won the lottery, then gives everyone a copy of the Four C's card, paper, and a pencil and asks them to write on the card what Car they would purchase; what Country they would visit; what Cuisine they would order on their vacation to that country (food does not have to match country);

and, finally, what Celebrity they would choose to have dinner with (a "Celebrity" is defined as a name recognizable by the general public).

Participants are told to print their answers on their cards and give them to a designated person within their subgroups.

The designated person then redistributes the cards and each person reads the card he or she has received out loud.

The trainer tells everyone to guess whose card is being read and to write their guesses on the sheet of paper.

Next, all the cards are read a second time; this time, individuals point to the person they think wrote the card as it is read. The person who wrote the card then identifies himself or herself. Participants keep track of how many of their guesses are correct.

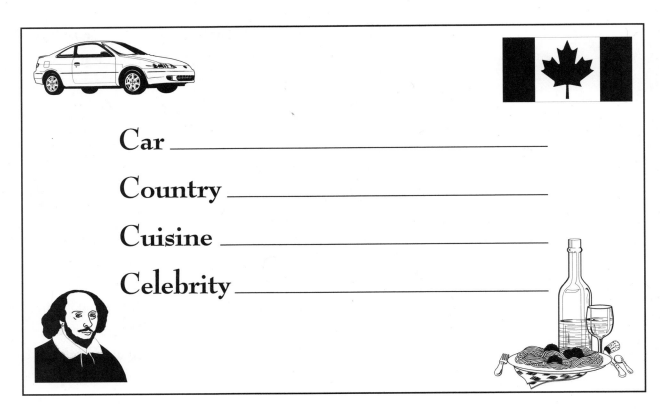

Car _____

Country _____

Cuisine _____

Celebrity _____

Car _____

Country _____

Cuisine _____

Celebrity _____

Four C's Template

Four-Quadrant Name Tent

- ☑ Icebreaker
- ☐ Networker
- ☐ Team Builder
- ☐ Task Tension
- ☑ Relationship Tension
- ☐ Personal Tension
- ☑ Focus Activity

Objectives
Break the ice
Become better acquainted
Provide focus on the topic

Class Length
Three hours or longer

Audience
Any

Group Size
Any group of twelve or more, in subgroups of five to seven

Time
10 to 15 minutes

Equipment
A copy of the name tent sample on an overhead transparency
One copy of the name tent template for each person
A pen or fine-point marker for each person

Process
The trainer gives each participant a copy of the Four-Quadrant Name Tent and asks everyone to fold the paper into thirds, making a triangular name tent. He or she displays the sample on an overhead projector. The "front" of the name tent is for the participant to decorate and insert his or her name.

The back of the tent is divided into four "window panes," in which participants are to write (or draw) four things about themselves, one in each pane. These items could be about one's personal life, professional life, family life, a talent, an interest, best vacation spot, favorite sport, and so forth.

Participants are asked not to share while they are writing, but to wait until all their panes are filled.

The trainer debriefs the activity with everyone in the room for a smaller group or in teams for a larger group.

Front

Back

(likes to golf)

(likes to travel)

(likes to read)

(has 6 children)

Sample Four-Quadrant Name Tent

NAME

COMPANY NAME

Four-Quadrant Name Tent Template

Gift Opener

☑	Icebreaker
☐	Networker
☑	Team Builder
☑	Task Tension
☑	Relationship Tension
☐	Personal Tension
☑	Focus Activity

Objectives   Break the ice
Allow opportunities to build teams
Relieve tension associated with a topic
Become better acquainted
Provide focus on the topic

Class Length   One day or longer

Audience   Any

Group Size   Twenty or fewer

Time   15 minutes

Equipment   A flip-chart sheet and markers for each subgroup
A large shoe box for each subgroup
Wrapping paper and ribbon
Several pairs of scissors and rolls of cellophane tape placed at convenient locations

Process   At the beginning of the class, the trainer asks participants to form small groups to brainstorm their expectations for the class as a "scribe" lists them on flip-chart sheets.

When the groups have finished this task, the trainer asks that the lists be folded and placed in a large shoe box, one per team.

Then the trainer asks participants to wrap and decorate the package and put it on display in the front of the room (or it can be put away for safekeeping if it is a longer class).

At the end of the day or class, the trainer unwraps the packages and participants go over the lists to see what has been covered and what still needs to be addressed.

Group Milling

- ☑ Icebreaker
- ☑ Networker
- ☐ Team Builder
- ☐ Task Tension
- ☑ Relationship Tension
- ☐ Personal Tension
- ☑ Focus Activity

Objectives Break the ice
Allow opportunities to network
Become better acquainted
Provide focus on the topic

Class Length Three hours or longer

Audience Any

Group Size Up to one hundred

Time 8 to 10 minutes

Equipment An 8½"x 11" sheet of paper per person for name tents
One medium-tip marker per person

Process The trainer hands out paper and markers as participants arrive and asks them to create graphic name tents without speaking with one another.

The graphic can be any item of the trainer's choice, for example, something of personal interest, a fact about the person, or an idea a participant plans to use.

When everyone has finished, the trainer asks everyone to stand up and move around the room, mingling with others by showing their graphic name tents, but only by nodding and smiling, *not speaking*.

Next the trainer gives an auditory signal to stop mingling for a minute. He or she instructs participants that they may now shake hands with others as they mingle, but still may not talk.

After a few minutes of mingling, the trainer tells everyone they may say, "Good morning" (or afternoon), state their names, and ask: "What did you draw on your name tent?" as they meet others.

After a few more minutes, the trainer debriefs the experience and begins the day's session.

Hail to the Chief

- ☑ Icebreaker
- ☐ Networker
- ☑ Team Builder
- ☐ Task Tension
- ☑ Relationship Tension
- ☐ Personal Tension
- ☑ Focus Activity

Objectives
Break the ice
Allow opportunities to build teams
Become better acquainted
Provide focus on the topic

Class Length
One day or longer

Audience
People from the same organization

Group Size
Any number, in subgroups of five to seven

Time
10 minutes

Equipment
Slips of paper with celebrity names (dead or alive/real or fictional) written on them (prepared in advance by the trainer)
A container for the slips of paper
A list of famous people or celebrities

Process
NOTE: This opener works best during multiple-day training when all participants are with the same organization and are generally acquainted with one another.

Prior to the class, the trainer prepares slips of paper with the names of celebrities on them (alive or dead/real or fictional) and puts them into a container.

After subgroups have been formed, the trainer asks one person from each table (or team) to draw a slip of paper.

The trainer asks each team to imagine that the person whose name was drawn is going to be the new president of the company. The team must then come up with ways that person would change the organization, both specifically and in general. For instance: "How would Madonna, as president, change your company?" "What if Bugs Bunny were president?" "If Bruce Wayne (Batman) were president of your company, what would be done differently?" Both positive and negative items should be brainstormed and discussed.

Hands Full

Objectives Break the ice
Allow opportunities to build teams
Relieve tension associated with a topic
Become better acquainted
Provide focus on the topic

Class Length One day or longer

Audience Any, but especially effective for groups that work within the same organization

Group Size Twelve or more

Time 5 minutes

Equipment One five-gallon wash tub or similar receptacle that will hold water
One permanent marker for the trainer
Twenty-five to thirty ping-pong balls

Process Prior to the class, the trainer fills a large tub with water.

After the group has assembled, the trainer asks participants to name their various job responsibilities. As each responsibility is named, the trainer writes the name of the responsibility and the person on a ping-pong ball and tosses it into the water.

When all of the ping-pong balls are in the water, the trainer asks for two volunteers to try to hold the balls under the water.

As the balls keep popping up, the trainer asks more participants, one at a time, to help, until enough participants are working together to hold all the balls under the water.

The trainer debriefs quickly, making the point that everyone must work together to manage all the responsibilities.

Human Scavenger Hunt

☑ Icebreaker

☑ Networker

☐ Team Builder

☐ Task Tension

☑ Relationship Tension

☐ Personal Tension

☑ Focus Activity

Objectives Break the ice
Allow opportunities to network
Become better acquainted
Provide focus on the topic

Class Length One day or longer

Audience Any

Group Size Fifteen to twenty

Time 10 to 15 minutes

Equipment One copy of the Scavenger Hunt List for each participant

Process *NOTE:* This activity works well after a getting acquainted exercise.

The trainer gives participants copies of the Scavenger Hunt List and extends the break to allow enough time for everyone to find people who match the items listed. Many other items could be added that were specific to the topic at hand, if desired.

Scavenger Hunt

1. Birthday in same quarter as yours
2. Night owl
3. Early bird
4. Born in the same state
5. Same color hair
6. Same color eyes
7. Right-handed
8. Left-handed
9. Likes food hot and spicy
10. Loves chocolate
11. Fluent in a second language
12. Has read a book in the last quarter
13. Has been outside the country in the last year
14. Owns a dog
15. Owns a cat
16. Owns a pet other than a dog or cat
17. Has two or more children
18. Has grandchildren
19. Has seen a play in the last quarter
20. Has seen a movie in the last week
21. Lives in an apartment
22. Lives in a condominium
23. Lives in a townhouse
24. Lives in a single-family home
25. Has been married more than ten years

Scavenger Hunt List

Interview the Trainer

- ☑ Icebreaker
- ☐ Networker
- ☐ Team Builder
- ☑ Task Tension
- ☑ Relationship Tension
- ☐ Personal Tension
- ☑ Focus Activity

Objectives Break the ice
Relieve tension associated with a topic
Become better acquainted
Provide focus on the topic

Class Length Ninety minutes or longer

Audience Any

Group Size Any number, in subgroups of five to seven

Time 6 to 10 minutes

Equipment None

Process *NOTE:* The point of this activity is to create a more relaxed atmosphere by helping the participants learn things about the trainer and the class.

After brief introductory remarks, the trainer invites the participants to interview him or her, saying something like: "For the next four or five minutes, you can interview me. Ask anything you like about me or the course, and I'll answer as best I can."

If people seem hesitant to ask questions, the trainer can have them brainstorm lists of questions in small groups for one or two minutes. This process will be less intimidating to the participants and will generate more questions.

The "Intro" You Deserve

☑ Icebreaker
☐ Networker
☐ Team Builder
☐ Task Tension
☑ Relationship Tension
☐ Personal Tension
☑ Focus Activity

Objectives Break the ice
Become better acquainted
Provide focus on the topic

Class Length Three hours or longer

Audience Any

Group Size Any number, in subgroups of five to seven

Time 10 minutes

Equipment A flip chart and markers with information about the trainer prepared in advance and folded back to be used later
A piece of paper for each participant
Pens or pencils for each participant

Process For this opener, the trainer arranges his or her own introduction by listing every possible item that could be of any interest whatsoever to participants on the flip chart or a piece of paper.

If no one from outside the class is available to handle the introduction, the trainer has one of the participants who arrives early read through the material that's been prepared and then present the trainer to the rest of the class.

Then the trainer asks each participant to create a minimum of five statements that would be part of "the intro YOU deserve," write them on their sheets of paper, and share their own introductions within small groups.

Option The trainer can have participants pair off and introduce each other to the rest of the group using the statements they have created.

BONUS!

Key Questions

☐ Icebreaker
☐ Networker
☑ Team Builder
☐ Task Tension
☑ Relationship Tension
☐ Personal Tension
☑ Focus Activity

Objectives Allow opportunities to build teams
Become better acquainted
Provide focus on the topic

Class Length Three hours or longer

Audience Any group that has some resistance to attending the training session

Group Size Any number, in subgroups of five to seven

Time 10 to 15 minutes

Equipment Paper and pencils for participants

Process *NOTE:* This exercise works best when preceded by a quick icebreaker. When faced with an audience that is attending the session "under protest," the trainer can use this type of key question exercise to help break down resistance to training.

The trainer gives out paper and pencils and asks participants to list two things they dislike about attending the training. When they have finished, the trainer asks them to write down two possible benefits that could come out of the training.

Then the trainer asks everyone to share their items in small groups and to report three areas they discussed to the large group.

The trainer debriefs the activity, asking the key question: "How can we overcome what we dislike about attending this session and focus on the possible benefits to us and our organization?"

☑	Icebreaker
☑	Networker
☐	Team Builder
☐	Task Tension
☑	Relationship Tension
☐	Personal Tension
☑	Focus Activity

Let's Get Acquainted

Objectives
Break the ice
Allow opportunities to network
Become better acquainted
Provide focus on the topic

Class Length
Three hours or longer

Audience
Any

Group Size
Any number under thirty, in subgroups of five to seven

Time
12 to 15 minutes

Equipment
One 3" x 5" index card for each person
A pencil for each person

Process
After the basic introduction to the session, the trainer hands out an index card and pencil for each person and announces: "We need to know four things about one another: your name, one fact about yourself that is important to you, why you are attending this class, and one thing you hope to gain from this class."

The trainer asks everyone to write the four pieces of information on their index cards and then to find someone in the room they do not know, or at least do not know well, and pair up. (If odd numbers are involved, the trainer can join one of the participants.)

The trainer goes first (even if not partnered with someone else) and shares his or her information, then asks partners to take turns sharing their partners' four pieces of information with the total group.

Option   If the class is larger than twenty, the trainer might break the class into two groups of about ten each.

Let's Share

☑	Icebreaker
☐	Networker
☐	Team Builder
☐	Task Tension
☑	Relationship Tension
☐	Personal Tension
☑	Focus Activity

Objectives   Break the ice
Become better acquainted
Provide focus on the topic

Class Length   Ninety minutes or longer

Audience   Any

Group Size   Any number, in subgroups of five to seven

Time   10 minutes

Equipment   A flip chart prepared by the trainer prior to the class
A copy of the sharing worksheet for each participant
Pencils for all participants

Process   To increase participants' willingness to share data and experiences about themselves, the trainer opens with a prepared flip-chart sheet on which he or she has listed five or six personal items, such as number of children or siblings, likes or dislikes, hobbies, educational background, and so forth.

The trainer shares these items with the group, then gives everyone a sharing sheet to fill out and a pencil.

When everyone has finished writing on their sheets, the trainer asks them to form small groups and share their information with one another.

Let's Share Worksheet

Instructions: Choose five or six of the following and write in your answers.

1. Married or single

2. Children: number, names, ages

3. Jobs worked as a teenager

4. Childhood nickname(s)

5. Favorite sport/hobby

6. Favorite spectator sport

7. Best vacation taken

8. Like/dislike

9. Favorite food

10. Schools attended

11. Places lived

12.

13.

14.

15.

Lifeline

☑	Icebreaker
☐	Networker
☐	Team Builder
☐	Task Tension
☑	Relationship Tension
☐	Personal Tension
☑	Focus Activity

Objectives   Break the ice
Become better acquainted
Provide focus on the topic

Class Length   Three hours or longer

Audience   Any group that will be working closely together in the future

Group Size   Any number, in subgroups of five to seven

Time   10 to 15 minutes

Equipment   An overhead transparency or flip chart and markers for the trainer
A sheet of paper and a pencil for each participant

Process   NOTE: Before beginning, the trainer should explain what the activity is about and allow people to opt out if they do not want to share life-changing, traumatic events with others. The process works best when the trainer models it by sharing his or her own life-changing events with the group by using a piece of flip-chart paper or an overhead transparency.

The trainer tells participants to draw a horizontal line across the middle of a piece of paper and to label the far left end of the line "birth" and the far right end of the line with the "day's date."

The trainer explains that the participants are to draw five vertical lines at any point along the horizontal line and to write a date on each line corresponding with a significant and life-changing event that occurred at that time.

When everyone has chosen dates and events, the trainer asks participants to share the significant events with their team members.

M & M®s

☑	Icebreaker
☐	Networker
☑	Team Builder
☑	Task Tension
☑	Relationship Tension
☐	Personal Tension
☑	Focus Activity

Objectives Break the ice
Allow opportunities to build teams
Relieve tension associated with a topic
Become better acquainted
Provide focus on the topic

Class Length One day or longer

Audience Any

Group Size Any number, in subgroups of five to seven

Time 5 to 10 minutes

Equipment One bowl or small basket per small group
Three to six M & M®s of different colors per participant

Process *NOTE:* This works well to open an afternoon or evening session. The trainer prepares a dish of multi-colored M & Ms for each sub-group and asks a representative of each group to take a dish back to where the group is sitting.

The trainer explains that each participant is to select three to six pieces of candy and line them up in a row.

Participants are told that they will be sharing one "item" per M & M with the others.

The trainer states the criteria for sharing: review points from the morning session; personal information; things that contribute to their job satisfaction; or a good idea no one has yet mentioned.

Everyone shares and eats the candy.

Option The trainer can prepare a chart according to color: one personal item shared for each red M & M, one job-related item for each orange M & M, etc.

Metaphor Opener

☑	Icebreaker
☐	Networker
☑	Team Builder
☑	Task Tension
☑	Relationship Tension
☐	Personal Tension
☑	Focus Activity

Objectives Break the ice
Allow opportunities to build teams
Relieve tension associated with a topic
Become better acquainted
Provide focus on the topic

Class Length Ninety minutes or longer

Audience Any

Group Size Any number, in subgroups of five to seven

Time 5 to 10 minutes at the beginning of a session

Equipment A list of open-ended sentences for each person, prepared in advance
A transparency or flip chart with the directions, prepared in advance
Flip-chart paper for posting answers (optional)
Felt-tipped markers (optional)

Process In advance of the class, the trainer prepares a list of open-ended sentences that use metaphors and copies enough for each participant. These sentences can be entirely related to the course, not at all related to the course, or a combination. For example, if the topic is "customer service," there may be from four to ten sentence completions.

Each sentence takes the following form:

Topic is like *noon* because. . . .

For example:

Training is like the comic pages because. . . .

Customer service is like a great breakfast because. . . .

Leadership is like a pie because. . . .

Sales is like training for a marathon because. . . .

Quality is like a leaky faucet because. . . .

The trainer asks participants to work with others to complete each sentence stem and challenges groups to complete each in as many ways as possible.

Option   The trainer may have the participants post the sentence completions they like most on a flip chart.

Musical Teams

<table>
<tr><td>☑</td><td>Icebreaker</td></tr>
<tr><td>☑</td><td>Networker</td></tr>
<tr><td>☐</td><td>Team Builder</td></tr>
<tr><td>☐</td><td>Task Tension</td></tr>
<tr><td>☑</td><td>Relationship Tension</td></tr>
<tr><td>☐</td><td>Personal Tension</td></tr>
<tr><td>☑</td><td>Focus Activity</td></tr>
</table>

Objectives   Break the ice
Allow opportunities to network
Become better acquainted
Provide focus on the topic

Class Length   Three hours or longer

Audience   Any

Group Size   Twenty to fifty

Time   10 to 15 minutes

Equipment   Four flip-chart sheets labeled A, B, C, and D in advance by the trainer
Masking tape for the trainer
A chart of suggested sorts for the trainer

Process   *NOTE:* In this version of "musical chairs" teams change rapidly, so make sure you have plenty of room to move around and (ideally) somewhere that participants may leave their personal items until final teams are formed.

The trainer hangs each of the four prepared flip-chart sheets in a different corner of the room.

Participants are all asked to stand and choose a corner of the room as the trainer calls out various criteria, for example, he or she may say, "If your favorite food is Italian, please go to corner A; if it's Mexican go to corner B; if it's Southern, go to corner C," and so forth.

The trainer gives participants two or three minutes to introduce themselves and network before calling out different criteria for grouping, for example: "If you like cats, go to corner A; if you prefer dogs, go to corner B; if you love both, go to corner C; if you'd rather have neither, go to corner D." Again, the trainer gives participants a few minutes to introduce and network before asking them to choose a different corner.

Trainers may use as many criteria as needed to get a good mix going.

Options   The trainer may show the choices on an overhead.

The final question may pertain to something about the topic, if desired.

	A	B	C	D
Food	Mexican	Italian	American	Other
Music	Rock	Jazz	Both	Neither
Pets	Dog	Cat	Both	Neither
Sports	Football	Baseball	Hockey	Basketball
Work	Planning	Organizing	Executing	Follow-Up

Sample Musical Team Sorts

My Hopes

- [x] Icebreaker
- [ ] Networker
- [ ] Team Builder
- [ ] Task Tension
- [x] Relationship Tension
- [ ] Personal Tension
- [x] Focus Activity

Objectives   Break the ice
Become better acquainted
Provide focus on the topic

Class Length   Ninety minutes or longer

Audience   Any

Group Size   Any number, in subgroups of five to seven

Time   8 to 10 minutes

Equipment   Enough copies of the sample sheets reproduced on index stock so there is one card per person, or 3" by 5" index cards may be used
A pencil or pen for each participant
A transparency or flip-chart sheet with the instructions

Process   The trainer provides each participant with a "My Hope" card, copied onto card stock, and a pencil. The trainer then asks everyone to list some hopes that they hold: one hope for the world, one hope for the organization, one hope for his or her family, and one personal hope.

Participants are then told to share with other members of their small groups.

My Hope

One hope I have for the world is . . . _____

One hope I have for the organization is . . . _____

One hope I have for my family is . . . _____

One hope I have for myself is . . . _____

My Hope

One hope I have for the world is . . . _____

One hope I have for the organization is . . . _____

One hope I have for my family is . . . _____

One hope I have for myself is . . . _____

My Hope

One hope I have for the world is . . . _____

One hope I have for the organization is . . . _____

One hope I have for my family is . . . _____

One hope I have for myself is . . . _____

My Hopes Template

My Life As a TV Show

- ☑ Icebreaker
- ☐ Networker
- ☐ Team Builder
- ☑ Task Tension
- ☑ Relationship Tension
- ☐ Personal Tension
- ☑ Focus Activity

Objectives Break the ice
Relieve tension associated with a topic
Become better acquainted
Provide focus on the topic

Class Length Ninety minutes or longer

Audience Any

Group Size Any number, in subgroups of five to seven

Time 10 minutes

Equipment One copy of the TV show sheet for each person
Paper and pencils for participants

Process The trainer divides participants into small groups and hands out the list of TV shows and pencils for everyone.

The trainer asks each person to examine the list of TV shows from the past and present and to choose one that is like his or her life and jot down three to five reasons why this is true.

The trainer allows three to five minutes for participants to choose and to jot down their reasons. Participants then explain in their small groups why they chose the programs they did.

List of TV Shows, Past and Present

Wheel of Fortune	The Andy Griffith Show
Gunsmoke	Touched by an Angel
I Love Lucy	ER
Wings	Father Knows Best
Lost in Space	The Twilight Zone
Caroline in the City	The Streets of San Francisco
Star Trek	Friends
Grace Under Fire	As the World Turns
Gilligan's Island	The Honeymooners
M*A*S*H	Cheers
The Price Is Right	Jeopardy
Jeopardy	The Young and the Restless

BONUS!

Name Tent Anchor

- ☑ Icebreaker
- ☐ Networker
- ☐ Team Builder
- ☑ Task Tension
- ☑ Relationship Tension
- ☐ Personal Tension
- ☑ Focus Activity

Objectives
Break the ice
Relieve tension associated with a topic
Become better acquainted
Provide focus on the topic

Class Length
Three hours or longer

Audience
Any

Group Size
Any number, in subgroups of five to seven

Time
5 to 8 minutes

Equipment
One name tent per person produced from the template onto card stock
One felt-tipped marker per person
A prepared flip chart or transparency as an example

Process
NOTE: Most name tents have nothing on the back (the side facing toward the participant). Research shows the value of repeatedly reviewing/revisiting content, and name tents can be used for that purpose.

At the beginning of class, the trainer hands out name tents (made earlier from the template) and markers and asks participants to complete the front of the name tent (usually with one-inch-high first name, a half-inch high last name, and yet smaller department, company, etc.

Then the trainer tells participants to write, in their own handwriting (this is key), the most important things they want to gain from the training.

All during the class the learner's eye is caught by the information on the back of his or her name tent, particularly if the writing is done with colorful markers.

Option A variation would be to have learners add content to their name tents at intervals during the training as key ideas or concepts are presented.

1.

2.

3.

4.

5.

NAME

Name Tent Anchor Template

![BONUS!]

Name Tent for Class "Ownership"

☑	Icebreaker
☐	Networker
☑	Team Builder
☑	Task Tension
☑	Relationship Tension
☐	Personal Tension
☑	Focus Activity

Objectives Break the ice
Allow opportunities to build teams
Relieve tension associated with a topic
Become better acquainted
Provide focus on the topic

Class Length Three hours or longer

Audience Any

Group Size Any number, in subgroups of five to seven

Time 8 to 10 minutes

Equipment Paper and pencils for all participants
One name tent on card stock per person copied from the template
One felt-tipped marker per person
One flip-chart sheet or transparency of the name tent template

Process *NOTE:* One of Pike's Laws is: "People don't argue with their own data." If a trainer hands participants a list of house rules, there can be resentment, but if participants create their own, they feel "ownership" over the process, especially when the rules are written on their name tents. This is a very effective exercise. Combining it with another "ownership" activity can prove especially effective.

The trainer begins by asking, "Have you ever been in a classroom in which instructor or participant behaviors ruined the class for you?" (Nods will occur.)

The trainer then asks that participants work together in small teams to create "ideal house rules," noting only that the hours spent and class content cannot be changed. The trainer offers an example, such as "respect ideas of others" and writes it on the transparency or flip chart.

Each team then shares its rules with the others. The rules with which all agree are written on everyone's name tents. By having the rules on the back of the tents, the participants are reminded of a commitment they made.

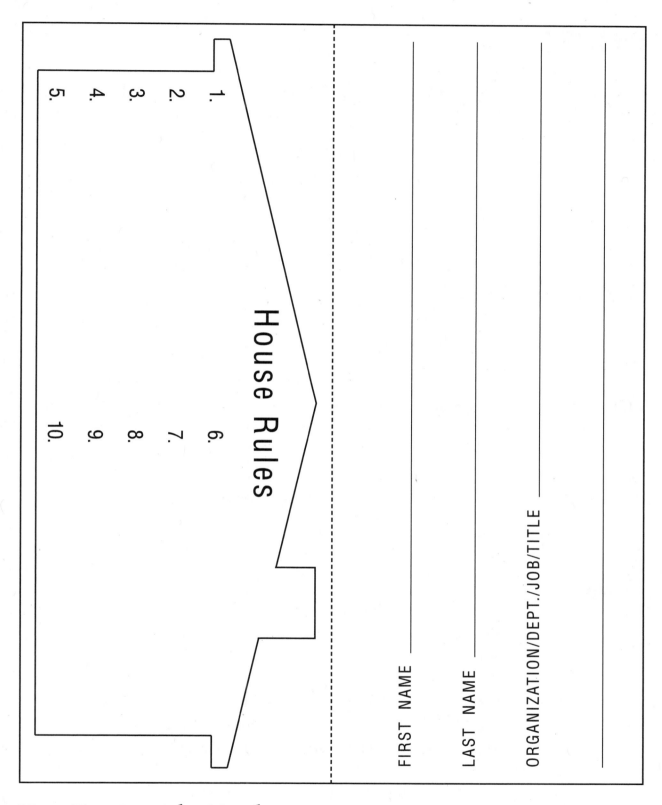

Name Tent Ownership Template

BONUS!

Name Tent Interview

- ☑ Icebreaker
- ☑ Networker
- ☐ Team Builder
- ☐ Task Tension
- ☑ Relationship Tension
- ☐ Personal Tension
- ☑ Focus Activity

Objectives Break the ice
Allow opportunities to network
Become better acquainted
Provide focus on the topic

Class Length Three hours or longer

Audience Any

Group Size Any number, in subgroups of five to seven

Time 8 to 10 minutes

Equipment One name tent per person, created on card stock from the template
One felt-tipped marker per person
Flip-chart sheet or transparency with an example of a filled-in name tent

Process The trainer gives each person a blank name tent, reproduced on card stock, and a marker and tells people to choose partners. (In odd-numbered classes, the trainer pairs with a participant.)

The trainer tells participants to create name tents for their partners by printing their partners' names on one side as the person would like to be addressed in class and filling in the information on the other side about their partners.

After everyone has finished, the trainer has everyone share his or her partner's information within subgroups or with the entire group in smaller classes.

Goal for class _____

What would make it a disaster? _____

Where were you born? _____

Where do you live? _____

Greatest job satisfaction _____

NAME _____

Name Tent Interview Template

BONUS!

Name Tent Spoof

☑	Icebreaker
☐	Networker
☑	Team Builder
☐	Task Tension
☑	Relationship Tension
☐	Personal Tension
☑	Focus Activity

Objectives Break the ice
Provide opportunities to build teams
Become better acquainted
Provide focus on the topic

Class Length Three hours or longer

Audience Any

Group Size Any number, in subgroups of five to seven

Time 5 to 10 minutes

Equipment Two name tags per person
Markers available for everyone to use

Process *NOTE:* If a trainer has difficulty remembering participant names, even when name tents are used, the trainer might begin a class by also asking participants to put their first names only, large and bold, on name tags and to wear them for the first few hours of the class. When name tags are used, the trainer can see the face of the learner and his or her name at a glance and learn names more quickly. It is also helpful for others when learners are out of their chairs and away from their name tents. The trainer can explain why both tents and tags are desired.

For this activity, the trainer asks participants each to prepare a second name tag, listing two things about themselves that are true and one that is not (a spoof). The trainer tells them to affix the second name tag and then form small groups, with teammates guessing which item is the spoof.

Options   The participants may also be instructed to move around the room trying to guess which of the items on others' name tags are spoofs.

At breaks, conversation and laughter grow out of the almost irresistible urge to guess which one of the three items is a spoof on others' name tags.

BONUS!

Name Tent Visual

- ☑ Icebreaker
- ☐ Networker
- ☐ Team Builder
- ☐ Task Tension
- ☑ Relationship Tension
- ☐ Personal Tension
- ☑ Focus Activity

Objectives Break the ice
Become better acquainted
Provide focus on the topic

Class Length Three hours or longer

Audience Any

Group Size Any number, in subgroups of five to seven

Time 5 to 8 minutes

Equipment One name tent per participant (copied from the template onto card stock)
One felt-tipped marker per person
One flip-chart sheet or transparency of the name tent template

Process *NOTE:* Because name tents face the trainer and other participants, the learner looks at the back of the name tent. It is therefore effective to use the back of the name tent for content and to use the front not only for names but to make a visual statement and share personal information.

The trainer hands out name tents and markers and asks each participant to put his or her name on the front of the name tent, leaving room in the four corners for additional information.

The trainer selects four things that can be added to the name tent as visuals. These can be job related, personal, or a mixture, ranging from state of birth to years with the organization (see the examples that follow). The trainer gives participants time to complete their four visuals and then allows time for everyone to display and share the information either with partners or in groups.

The visual serves to remind others of what each person has shared. It is especially valuable if team membership changes, as the name tents move with the people.

Possible Visuals:

Outline or name of state

Greatest job satisfaction/challenge

Place of birth

Number of children/siblings

Greatest job strength

Best/dream vacation spot

Favorite food/hobby

Years with company/department

Favorite sport/team

Number of times moved/cars owned

Favorite music/movie/book

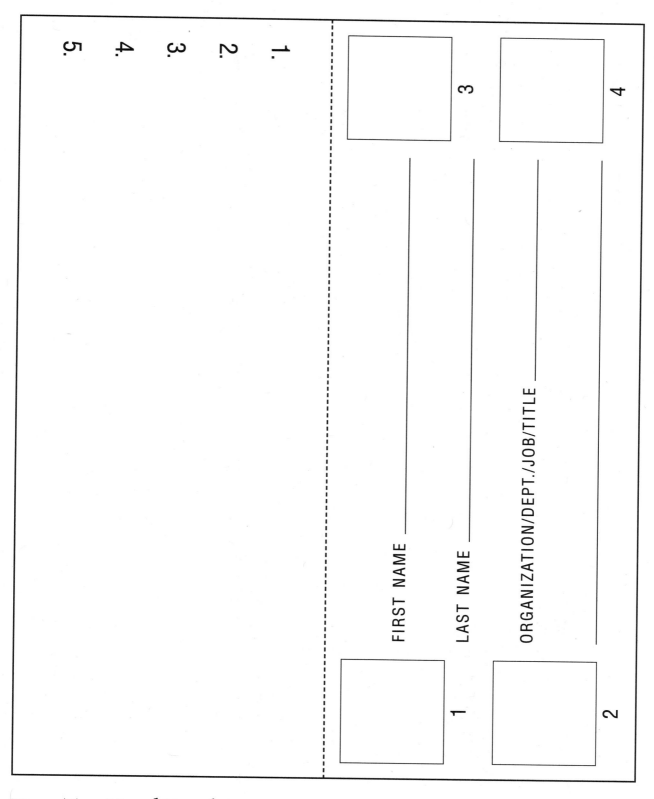

Name Tent Visual Template

Nicknames

- ☑ Icebreaker
- ☐ Networker
- ☐ Team Builder
- ☐ Task Tension
- ☑ Relationship Tension
- ☐ Personal Tension
- ☑ Focus Activity

Objectives Break the ice
Become better acquainted
Provide focus for the topic

Class Length Ninety minutes or longer

Audience Any

Group Size Any number, in subgroups of five to seven

Time 5 to 10 minutes

Equipment Two adhesive-backed name tags per person
One felt-tipped marker per person

Process The trainer gives each person two name tags and a marker and asks everyone to write his or her name on one of the tags and wear it.

The trainer tells participants to write a nickname they have been called at some point during their lives on the other name tag. (Those who hated their nicknames or those who never had one are allowed to make up one they would like to have had.)

The trainer then asks participants to introduces themselves to their teammates both by name and by nickname and to explain where they picked up the nickname (or why they would like to have had a particular one).

BONUS!

Other Half Interview

☑ Icebreaker
☑ Networker
☐ Team Builder
☐ Task Tension
☑ Relationship Tension
☑ Personal Tension
☑ Focus Activity

Objectives Break the ice
Allow opportunities to network
Become better acquainted
Alleviate personal tension
Provide focus on the topic

Class Length Three hours or longer

Audience Any

Group Size Up to fifty, in subgroups of five to seven

Time 10 to 20 minutes

Equipment One Other Half Interview form per person
A pencil or pen for each person
One name tent per person made from the template and prepared with half of a "famous pair" written on the underside
One felt-tipped marker per person

Process Prior to the class, the trainer prepares an interview form with questions that are appropriate for an icebreaker with that particular group. The trainer also prepares name tents from the template, writing the name of half of a famous pair on the inside of each one and placing the tents on the tables so that pairs will not be sitting together.

As participants come to the class, they are given interview forms, pens or pencils, and felt-tipped markers.

Once all participants are seated, the trainer asks them to fill out their own names on the name tents and then to look inside, where they will find the name of half of a well-known pair.

Participants are asked to mingle, find their other half, and introduce themselves. They then interview their partners, fill out the forms, and introduce one another to the group.

Sample Pairs

Ham/Eggs

Batman/Robin

Laurel/Hardy

Green Hornet/Kato

Salt/Pepper

Humphrey Bogart/Lauren Bacall

Hot/Cold

Road Runner/Wiley Coyote

George Burns/Gracie Allen

Bugs Bunny/Elmer Fudd

Donnie Osmond/Marie Osmond

Mickey Mouse/Minnie Mouse

Spencer Tracy/Kathryn Hepburn

Sugar/Spice

Mark McGwire/Sammy Sosa

Richard Nixon/Henry Kissinger

Minneapolis/St. Paul

FIRST NAME _____

LAST NAME _____

ORGANIZATION/DEPT./JOB/TITLE _____

Famous Pairs

1. Where were you born? _____
2. Favorite class in school? _____
3. How long with the organization? _____
4. How long in present job? _____
5. Favorite hobby? _____
6. Favorite sport? _____
7. Dream vacation? _____
8. Greatest challenge? _____

9. What do you like best about your job? _____
10. Last movie seen? _____
11. Favorite book? _____
12. Favorite music? _____
13. Favorite actor/actress? _____
14. Married? _____
15. Children? _____
    Boy/Girl/Ages _____

Other Half Interview Template

Personalized Coat of Arms

☑ Icebreaker
☐ Networker
☐ Team Builder
☐ Task Tension
☑ Relationship Tension
☐ Personal Tension
☑ Focus Activity

Objectives Break the ice
Become better acquainted
Provide focus on the topic

Class Length Three hours or longer

Audience Any

Group Size Any number, in subgroups of five to seven

Time 15 to 20 minutes

Equipment One copy of the Coat of Arms for each participant
Several fine-point felt-tipped markers for each participant
Masking tape

Process The trainer gives a copy of the Coat of Arms and a fine-point marker to each person and tells them to make a drawing that represents an interest they might hold in one of the segments.

When everyone has finished, the trainer tells them to draw a symbol that represents their family in the segment diagonally opposite from the one they have just filled in.

Then the trainer instructs everyone to use words to fill in one of the empty segments with items such as three things the person likes best about his or her job; city and state of birth; favorite movie, book, or TV show; and so on.

The trainer tells everyone to fill the final segment with three things he or she hopes to get out of the training session and to decorate the coat of arms so that it can be displayed for other participants to see.

The participants are told to discuss what they have written in their subgroups.

1.

2.

3.

4.

Playing Card Introduction

- ☑ Icebreaker
- ☑ Networker
- ☐ Team Builder
- ☐ Task Tension
- ☑ Relationship Tension
- ☐ Personal Tension
- ☑ Focus Activity

Objectives   Break the ice
Allow opportunities to network
Become better acquainted
Provide focus on the topic

Class Length   Three hours or longer

Audience   Any

Group Size   Any number, in subgroups of five to seven, although six is ideal

Time   8 to 12 minutes

Equipment   Introductory letters prepared and sent to participants prior to the class containing:
One list of interview questions per person
Half of a playing card per person

Process   *NOTE:* The approach used for this activity helps to ensure that the participants arrive on time to interview their partners and to be interviewed. It also gives everyone a partner to work with.

Prior to the class, the trainer sends letters to participants welcoming them to the class and reminding them of the time and location.

Included with the letter are a name tag and one half of a playing card. (If there may be a challenge with "no shows," the trainer waits until ten minutes before class to distribute the memos and cards.)

The trainer tells participants in the letter that they will be asked to introduce the person who has the other half of the card to the group, assuring them that they will have time to find the person at the beginning of the class.

The trainer also includes an interview sheet with sections such as name, company, department, and title, and some personal items such as a strengths, hobbies, marital status, and so forth. (Some samples are shown on page 13.)

Ragged Start

- [✓] Icebreaker
- [ ] Networker
- [✓] Team Builder
- [✓] Task Tension
- [✓] Relationship Tension
- [ ] Personal Tension
- [✓] Focus Activity

Objectives Break the ice
Allow opportunities to build teams
Relieve tension associated with a topic
Become better acquainted
Provide a focus on the topic

Class Length Three hours or longer

Audience Any

Group Size Any number, in subgroups of five to seven

Time 8 to 10 minutes

Equipment Copies of three or four mini case studies so that they can be handed out randomly, one per participant. (For a class of twenty-four participants, six copies each of four case studies or eight copies each of three case studies would be required.)

Process *NOTE:* This exercise gives participants an immediate topic of discussion and gives them a jump start on class content.

Prior to the class, the trainer prepares three or four mini case studies, based on session content.

As participants arrive, the trainer hands out copies of the case studies, one per person, and invites everyone to look them over and discuss them with others as they wait for class to start.

Random Numbers

- ☑ Icebreaker
- ☐ Networker
- ☐ Team Builder
- ☐ Task Tension
- ☑ Relationship Tension
- ☐ Personal Tension
- ☑ Focus Activity

Objectives
Break the ice
Become better acquainted
Provide focus on the topic

Class Length
One hour or longer

Audience
Any

Group Size
Any number, in subgroups of five to seven

Time
5 to 10 minutes

Equipment
One name tag per person
One sample chart or transparency of a name tag
Felt-tipped markers available for everyone to use

Process
As participants enter, the trainer gives each person a name tag and asks them to write their names and three random numbers, from 1 to 10, on their tags.

When the class begins, the trainer introduces himself or herself and explains the three numbers on his or her own tag. (For instance, if the numbers were 5, 2, and 8, the trainer might say that he or she has 5 pets, 2 cars, and an 8-mile drive to work or 5 sisters, 2 jobs, and ate Mexican food 8 times in the past month.)

Participants are then asked to introduce themselves and to come up with a reason for each of the numbers they chose. Because the numbers were randomly chosen, participants will need a moment or two to think of what the number might apply to before beginning to share.

Silly Hats

✓	Icebreaker
☐	Networker
☐	Team Builder
✓	Task Tension
✓	Relationship Tension
☐	Personal Tension
✓	Focus Activity

Objectives   Break the ice
Relieve tension associated with a topic
Become better acquainted
Provide focus on the topic

Class Length   One day or longer

Audience   Any group embarking on a new learning experience that may be perceived as threatening or unfamiliar

Group Size   Any number, in subgroups of five to seven

Time   10 to 15 minutes

Equipment   One or two pages from a newspaper for each person, including the trainer
One roll of tape per subgroup

Process   The trainer gives each person one or two pages from a newspaper and asks everyone to make hats.

The trainer also makes and wears a newspaper hat when introducing himself or herself to the group. Others are asked to do the same.

The trainer then makes the point that they will be trying on some new ideas during the class and that they may feel awkward, but that none of them will look any sillier than they do right now, so everyone can relax.

Silly Sentences

☑ Icebreaker
☐ Networker
☑ Team Builder
☑ Task Tension
☑ Relationship Tension
☐ Personal Tension
☑ Focus Activity

Objectives Break the ice
Allow opportunities to build teams
Relieve tension associated with a topic
Become better acquainted
Provide focus on the topic

Class Length Ninety minutes or longer

Audience Any

Group Size Any number, in subgroups of eight to twelve

Time 5 to 7 minutes

Equipment One flip-chart sheet per subgroup
One felt-tipped marker per participant
Masking tape

Process *NOTE:* This is particularly effective in groups that are resistant to activities that are construed as too frivolous.

Prior to the class, the trainer tapes a large sheet of newsprint to the wall for each subgroup.

Each participant is given a felt-tipped marker as he or she arrives.

The trainer divides the group into subgroups. Participants are asked to form a line at the appropriate sheet of newsprint and to write one word on the chart, in turn. The object is to have a sentence (with subjects, verbs, and punctuation), but *NO pre-planning* is allowed. Each member of the subgroup must contribute at least one word as rapidly as possible.

Option   A course-related topic can be written at the top of each sheet, and then the sentences must relate to that topic.

BONUS!

Six "H" Name Tent

- ☑ Icebreaker
- ☐ Networker
- ☐ Team Builder
- ☐ Task Tension
- ☑ Relationship Tension
- ☐ Personal Tension
- ☑ Focus Activity

Objectives Break the ice
Become better acquainted
Provide focus on the topic

Class Length Three hours or longer

Audience Any

Group Size Any number, in subgroups of five to seven

Time 10 to 15 minutes

Equipment One copy of the name tent template for each person, copied onto card stock
Fine-point felt-tipped markers

Process The trainer gives participants name tents and markers and tells them to write their names and the other information indicated on the front.

When everyone has finished, the trainer directs their attention to the six H's on the opposite side and asks them to fill in information about themselves under the categories there: Hobby, Habit, Hope, Holiday (a formal holiday such as the Fourth of July or Christmas), Hero/Hero-ine, and History (a significant date in one's own history).

When all name tents are complete, the participants are asked to share their information within their subgroups or with everyone if the group is small.

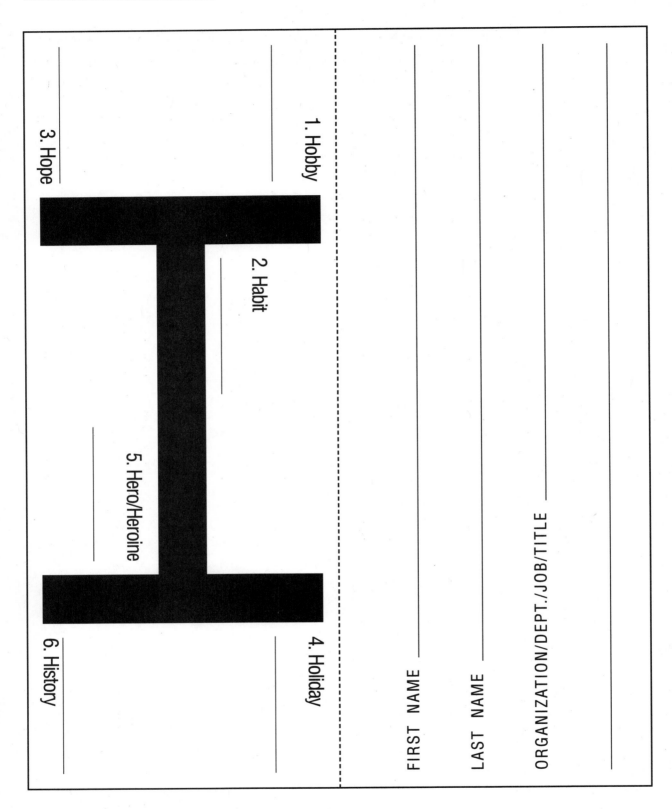

Six "H" Name Tent Template

BONUS!

Striptease

- ☑ Icebreaker
- ☐ Networker
- ☐ Team Builder
- ☐ Task Tension
- ☑ Relationship Tension
- ☐ Personal Tension
- ☑ Focus Activity

Objectives   Break the ice
Become better acquainted
Provide focus on the topic

Class Length   Ninety minutes or longer

Audience   Any

Group Size   Any number, in subgroups of five to seven

Time   8 to 10 minutes

Equipment   One name tag per person
One felt-tipped marker per person
One roll of clear tape per subgroup
Enough adjective strips cut from the template so that each person can choose four strips at random and there will be some left for each subgroup
One container per subgroup to hold the adjective strips

Process   Prior to the class, the trainer makes as many copies of the template as there are subgroups, cuts up one for each subgroup, and places the adjective strips in containers. The trainer also leaves a roll of clear tape for each subgroup.

As participants enter the room, the trainer hands out name tags and markers and tells them to write their names on the tags and then to draw four (or more, if desired) adjective strips at random from the container and affix them to their name tags.

Once the class has assembled, the trainer asks each person to introduce himself or herself and to explain how the adjectives they drew pertain to them. The description can be strictly tied to the workplace or can be anything the facilitator might wish to use (including home life, vacations, personality, etc.).

The trainer emphasizes that all adjectives must be given a positive slant, for example: "One of my words is 'stubborn.' When I am involved in fixing a problem, I stubbornly refuse to give up until a solution is reached."

After all participants have discussed how the adjectives fit them, they are asked to discuss not only what they have learned about themselves and their teammates, but also how words with "negative" connotation can be given a positive slant.

Enthusiastic	Cautious	Good Natured	Friendly
Accurate	Outspoken	Conventional	Decisive
Adventurous	Insightful	Persuasive	Observant
Tactful	Brave	Inspiring	Cheerful
Stimulating	Kind	Perceptive	Independent
Competitive	Logical	Loyal	Charming
Sociable	Patient	Self-Reliant	Thorough
Confident	Well-Disciplined	Persistent	Good Mixer
Contented	Cooperative	Direct	Even Tempered
Neighborly	Careful	Respectful	Optimistic

Striptease Template

Things You Carry

☑ Icebreaker
☐ Networker
☐ Team Builder
☐ Task Tension
☑ Relationship Tension
☐ Personal Tension
☑ Focus Activity

Objectives Break the ice
Become better acquainted
Provide focus on the topic

Class Length One hour or longer

Audience Any

Group Size Any number, in subgroups of five to seven

Time 5 to 7 minutes

Equipment None

Process The trainer asks participants to look in their wallets, purses, pockets, or briefcases and to pull out three or four items that would be unique to them, that is, something that no one else at the table would have or carry, for example, family pictures, a zoo membership card, mementos unique to the individual, a particular brand of lipstick, a special coin, and so forth. If two people in a group have the same item, then both must find a replacement.

The trainer then has subgroups discuss the following questions and leads a wrap-up discussion of the relevance of the activity:

1. How difficult was it to find "unique" items?

2. Did some people have an advantage? In what way?

3. What advantage is there in having people with different skills, knowledge, and experiences in a work group?

To Be a Success

☑ Icebreaker
☐ Networker
☑ Team Builder
☑ Task Tension
☑ Relationship Tension
☐ Personal Tension
☑ Focus Activity

Objectives Break the ice
Allow opportunities to build teams
Relieve tension associated with a topic
Become better acquainted
Provide focus on the topic

Class Length Ninety minutes or longer

Audience Any

Group Size Any number, in subgroups of two to six

Time 8 to 10 minutes

Equipment One pad of Post-it® Notes per person
Pens or pencils for all participants
Three flip-chart sheets, prepared in advance by the trainer
Masking tape

Process Prior to the class, the trainer hangs three flip-chart sheets on the wall, one labeled "Things We Can't Do Anything About in This Room," another labeled "Realistic," and another labeled "Unrealistic." The trainer covers the titles of the sheets by bringing the bottom of the sheet up and taping it loosely to the top.

The trainer divides the class into teams and asks them to brainstorm five things that they would like to have happen/to be learned/to take place in order to feel that the training session is a success.

The trainer hands out pens or pencils and gives each participant a Post-it® Note pad to write their answers, one per note. The participants are told to share their answers within their subgroups.

Then the trainer removes the masking tape from the flip-chart sheets and invites everyone to post their notes on the appropriate charts.

Throughout the class, the trainer checks back to the chart labeled "Realistic," so that it becomes the benchmark for success for the class.

"Tomorrow I'm Going to. . . ."

☑ Icebreaker
☐ Networker
☐ Team Builder
☑ Task Tension
☑ Relationship Tension
☐ Personal Tension
☑ Focus Activity

Objectives Break the ice
Relieve tension associated with a topic
Become better acquainted
Provide focus on the topic

Class Length Two hours or longer

Audience Any

Group Size Any number, in subgroups of five to seven

Time 8 to 10 minutes

Equipment One of each of the cards from the templates, copied onto different colored index stock and cut out
A pen or pencil for each person

Process The trainer gives each participant two different "tomorrow" cards and tells everyone to imagine (realistically) what they would do if they were to have a day off the next day and to record what they would do on the appropriate card.

Then the trainer tells them to fill out their second cards with reference to their jobs: "Tomorrow, if all goes perfectly at work. . . ."

Each participant is to write what he or she would have to achieve or accomplish and then share the information within their small groups.

Option   The work-related cards can be used to start "to-do" lists for the next day.

Tomorrow I'm going to . . .

Tomorrow I'm going to . . .

Tomorrow I'm going to . . .

Tomorrow I'm going to . . .

Tomorrow I'm going to . . .

Tomorrow I'm going to . . .

Tomorrow Card Template 1

Tomorrow if all goes perfectly at work . . .

Tomorrow if all goes perfectly at work . . .

Tomorrow if all goes perfectly at work . . .

Tomorrow if all goes perfectly at work . . .

Tomorrow if all goes perfectly at work . . .

Tomorrow if all goes perfectly at work . . .

Tomorrow Card Template 2

Toothpick Confessions

- ☑ Icebreaker
- ☐ Networker
- ☑ Team Builder
- ☐ Task Tension
- ☑ Relationship Tension
- ☐ Personal Tension
- ☑ Focus Activity

Objectives Break the ice
Allow opportunities to build teams
Become better acquainted
Provide focus on the topic

Class Length Ninety minutes or longer

Audience Any

Group Size Any number up to twelve; larger groups can be used with subgroups of ten or twelve

Time 5 to 8 minutes

Equipment Ten toothpicks per person

Process At the beginning of the class, the trainer gives each participant ten toothpicks, then asks each participant, in turn, to share something they have *never done*: for example, "I have never jaywalked" or "I have never traveled to Spain." After each statement, anyone in the group who *HAS* done the activity mentioned (that is, jaywalked or been to Spain) forfeits a toothpick.

Then the next person shares one thing he or she has never done. Disclosures continue until someone has lost all ten toothpicks.

Twenty Questions

☑ Icebreaker

☑ Networker

☐ Team Builder

☐ Task Tension

☑ Relationship Tension

☐ Personal Tension

☑ Focus Activity

Objectives Break the ice
Allow opportunities to network
Become better acquainted
Provide focus on the topic

Class Length One day or longer

Audience Any

Group Size Twelve to fifty, in subgroups of six or seven

Time 20 minutes

Equipment One name tag per person with a famous person's name written on it

Process Prior to the class, the trainer prepares one name tag per person with the name of a famous person on it, real or fictional, dead or alive (see the list accompanying this activity for nonfiction examples).

As participants enter the room, the trainer greets them, then places a name tag on each person's back. Everyone is told not to mention their name tags nor the ones that others are wearing until told to do so.

Once the class begins, the trainer asks participants to move around the room and introduce themselves to others, with the purpose to ask other participants twenty (or fewer) questions, one at a time, until everyone has determined the names written on the name tags on their backs.

Only one question may be asked at a time before moving to another person and questions must be phrased so that they can be answered by a "yes" or a "no" only.

The time allowed should be quite short (depending on the number of participants) to keep people moving. Once they have discovered who they are, participants are to return to their original seats.

Option The famous persons can be in groups of five to seven, such as movie stars, cartoon characters, baseball players, politicians, or whatever. When everyone has identified themselves, they can form subgroups by category.

Twenty Questions Sample Listing

Movie Stars

Marilyn Monroe

Humphrey Bogart

Katherine Hepburn

Bruce Willis

Mel Gibson

Tom Cruise

Presidents

George Washington

Abraham Lincoln

Thomas Jefferson

Teddy Roosevelt

Andrew Jackson

John F. Kennedy

Pro Athletes

Babe Ruth

Michael Jordan

Arnold Palmer

Barry Bonds

Kareem Abdul Jabbar

Wayne Gretsky

Composers

Bach

Beethoven

Vivaldi

Rachmaninoff

Strauss

Brahms

Singers

Whitney Houston

Michael Jackson

Michael Bolton

Mariah Carey

Mahaliah Jackson

Most Admired People

Billy Graham

Mother Teresa

Grace Kelly

Jacqueline Kennedy Onassis

Pope John Paul II

Bishop Fulton J. Sheen

☑ Icebreaker
☐ Networker
☐ Team Builder
☐ Task Tension
☑ Relationship Tension
☐ Personal Tension
☑ Focus Activity

Two, Three, and Four Things

Objectives   Break the ice
Become better acquainted
Provide focus on the topic

Class Length   Three hours or longer

Audience   Any

Group Size   Any number, in subgroups of five to seven

Time   10 minutes

Equipment   One Two, Three, and Four Things Form per person
A pencil or pen per person

Process   Prior to the class, the trainer makes enough copies of the form on the following page for each participant.

The trainer gives participants copies of the form and pens or pencils and instructs them to fill out their forms and share within their subgroups.

Two, Three, and Four Things Form

Two things I would change about myself:

1.

2.

Three things I accept about myself:

1.

2.

3.

Four things I like about myself:

1.

2.

3.

4.

Uniqueness and Commonalities

☑ Icebreaker
☐ Networker
☑ Team Builder
☐ Task Tension
☑ Relationship Tension
☐ Personal Tension
☑ Focus Activity

Objectives Break the ice
Allow opportunities to build teams
Become better acquainted
Provide focus on the topic

Class Length One day or longer

Audience Any

Group Size Any number, in subgroups of four to six

Time 10 minutes

Equipment Flip-chart paper and markers for each subgroup
A sample chart of unique or common aspects on a transparency or flip chart

Process *NOTE:* This exercise serves three purposes: (1) It builds a team through the completion of the task; (2) it serves as a tension reducer as areas in common are discovered; and (3) it serves as a very effective icebreaker.

The trainer forms subgroups of four to six people and assigns them to find four to six (depending on time) things they have in common with one another—things that are not obvious and could not be assumed, although they can be simple.

The trainer then assigns subgroups to discover one to three *positive* unique qualities that each individual has in relation to others on the team, for example, one person may speak Spanish, play the ukulele, or have traveled to Europe. The trainer should emphasize that the uniqueness must be positive.

Each subgroup then fills out a chart of its uniqueness on flip-chart paper, similar to the sample.

Options   Teams can verbally share this information with everyone in the room, rather than making a chart.

Each group can share the most interesting thing they have in common, rather than a difference.

Each group can choose the most interesting of the unique things they learned about others in the group.

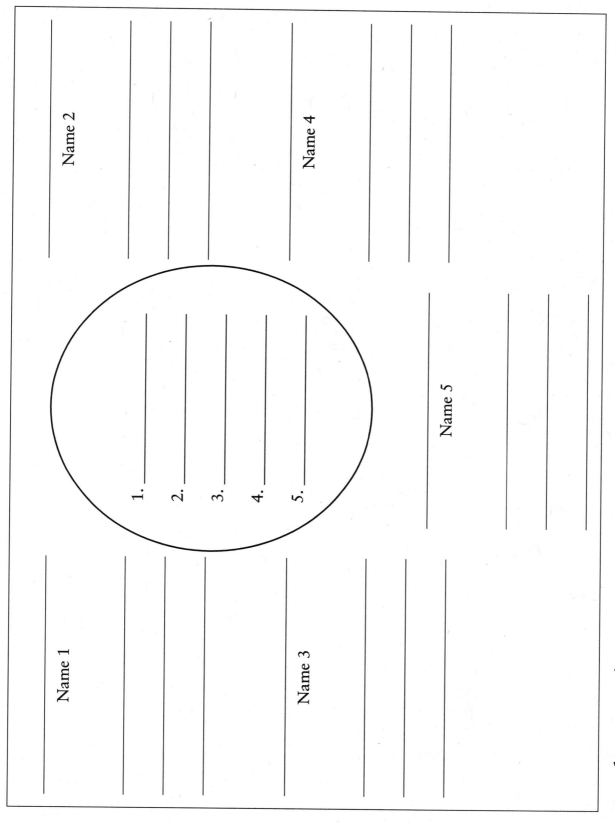

Sample Listing of Unique or Common Aspects

Unusual Props

- ☑ Icebreaker
- ☐ Networker
- ☑ Team Builder
- ☑ Task Tension
- ☑ Relationship Tension
- ☐ Personal Tension
- ☑ Focus Activity

Objectives Break the ice
Allow opportunities to build teams
Relieve tension associated with a topic
Become better acquainted
Provide focus on the topic

Class Length Three hours or longer

Audience Any

Group Size Any number, in subgroups of five to seven

Time 8 to 10 minutes

Equipment A variety of distinct and unusual props, such as stuffed animals, articles of clothing, vegetables, mirrors, or toys, one prop per team

Process *NOTE:* This activity works well when preceded by another quick icebreaker. Using creative props can help ease tension and stress in learning situations.

The trainer puts participants into teams and gives each team one of the props.

Teams are then asked to name their props and come up with three ways that they tie in with the content of the session and share with everyone in the class.

Unusual Request

Objectives   Break the ice
Relieve tension associated with a topic
Provide focus on the topic

Class Length   Three hours or longer

Audience   Any group meeting to learn something innovative or new

Group Size   Any number, in subgroups of five to seven

Time   5 to 7 minutes

Equipment   None

Process   *NOTE:* This activity should be preceded by an icebreaker.

The trainer, as a warmup to learning something that may make participants uncomfortable, asks everyone to stand up and to do something minor that may make them feel a bit uncomfortable. For example, the trainer may have everyone cross their arms as they usually do and then cross them differently by changing which arm is on top.

The trainer then forms teams to discuss the fact that they may have new experiences during the course, such as standing at an easel or speaking before a group for the first time, that are similar to new experiences they are about to have on the job. Discussions could cover, for example, the fact that new managerial behaviors are being learned and that the initial reaction has been resentment or resistance, or that some will try out new skills in the classroom but revert to old behavior that is more comfortable.

After the teams have discussed the issues, the trainer asks them to come up with two or three ways individuals could use to feel more comfortable when dealing with the discomfort of learning something new.

Vote Your Priorities

- ☐ Icebreaker
- ☐ Networker
- ☑ Team Builder
- ☑ Task Tension
- ☑ Relationship Tension
- ☐ Personal Tension
- ☑ Focus Activity

Objectives Allow opportunities to build teams
Relieve tension associated with a topic
Become better acquainted
Provide focus on the topic

Class Length Three hours or longer

Audience Any

Group Size Any number, in subgroups of five to seven

Time 8 to 10 minutes

Equipment Flip-chart sheets and markers for the trainer
A list of topics for each person, prepared in advance by the trainer
A supply of colored adhesive dots for each person or subgroup

Process Prior to the class, the trainer posts a flip-chart sheet divided with a vertical line. On the left side is a list of the topics to be covered and the right side is blank.

The trainer gives each participant an 8½" by 11" copy of the flip-chart sheet and asks everyone to select the three to five areas that are of most interest to him or her.

Then the trainer tells the teams to look for commonalities and use their colored dots to "vote," directly on the chart, to indicate the five or six topics of most importance to them as a team.

The trainer assures participants that all topics listed on the original sheet will be covered, but states that the "voting board" will be consulted for how much time will be devoted to a particular topic or issue.

The trainer can then expand or contract the amount of time and depth of treatment for each topic, based on the needs of the group.

What Can You Do with It?

☐	Icebreaker
☐	Networker
☑	Team Builder
☑	Task Tension
☑	Relationship Tension
☐	Personal Tension
☑	Focus Activity

Objectives Allow opportunities to build teams
Relieve tension associated with a topic
Become better acquainted
Provide focus on the topic

Class Length Three and one-half hours or longer

Audience Any audience learning material for which there may be resistance

Group Size Any number, in subgroups of five to seven

Time 8 to 10 minutes

Equipment A 3" x 5" index card with a "prop" written on it for each subgroup (see the list of sample props on the next page)
Optional: Actual props for each subgroup

Process *NOTE:* This activity is best when preceded by a quick icebreaker. If the content of the training involves problem solving or introduces change, this activity usually proves to be a mind opener for participants and helps them look at common things or "how things are" with new eyes.

Prior to the class, the trainer places a 3" x 5" index card on each table with the name of an object written on it that has no connection with the topic of the session. (See the list below.)

The trainer has participants form teams of five to seven people and then asks them to brainstorm as many uses as possible for the item listed on the card. The trainer stresses that they are to go for quantity, not quality.

At the end of the allotted time, each group leader gives a report to the large group, stating what their item was and the uses they found for it. The results usually include a lot of laughter, plus recognition of the versatility and creativity of the mind.

Option   The trainer may obtain actual offbeat props, place them in bags, and have each group select a bag before brainstorming uses for their prop.

Sample Props

Brick	Wire coat hanger
One-foot paint roller	Ball-point pen
Used tire	Toothbrush
Paper clip	Piece of string
Used chewing gum	Dead "C" battery
Light bulb	Stuffed animal
Tennis racket	Steering wheel
Computer keyboard	Empty paint can
Rake	Shovel
Child's toy	TV remote control
Wastebasket	Stapler
Clock	Lamp

What Would Your Best Friend Say?

☑	Icebreaker
☐	Networker
☐	Team Builder
☐	Task Tension
☑	Relationship Tension
☑	Personal Tension
☑	Focus Activity

Objectives Break the ice
Become better acquainted
Alleviate personal tension
Provide focus on the topic

Class Length One hour or longer

Audience Any

Group Size Any number, in subgroups of five to seven

Time 6 to 15 minutes

Equipment One 3" x 5" index card per person
One pen or pencil per person

Process The trainer asks participants to picture their best friends and then to imagine that someone has asked their friends to name the three best things about them (the participants). After a few moments of contemplation, the trainer asks them to write the three things on their index cards and then to share within their subgroups.

What's Your Line?

☑ Icebreaker
☐ Networker
☐ Team Builder
☐ Task Tension
☑ Relationship Tension
☐ Personal Tension
☑ Focus Activity

Objectives   Break the ice
Become better acquainted
Provide focus on the topic

Class Length   Three hours or longer

Audience   Any

Group Size   Any number, in subgroups of five to seven

Time   8 to 10 minutes

Equipment   Three blank name tags per person
One felt-tipped marker per person

Process   The trainer gives each participant three name tags and tells everyone to write his or her name with a bright marker on the first.

On the second name tag, the trainer tells people to write up to three pieces of information about themselves that is job related, such as department, length of time with the organization, job title, or major responsibility.

For the third name tag, the trainees are told to think back to their childhoods and recall up to three professions they once thought they might pursue, for example, race car driver, actor, astronaut, doctor, nurse, pilot, and so on, and to write this information on the name tag. When everyone has completed three name tags, the information is shared within subgroups.

What's Your Role?

☑	Icebreaker
☐	Networker
☐	Team Builder
☑	Task Tension
☑	Relationship Tension
☐	Personal Tension
☑	Focus Activity

Objectives Break the ice
Relieve tension associated with a topic
Become better acquainted
Provide focus on the topic

Class Length Three hours or longer

Audience Any

Group Size Any number, in subgroups of five to seven

Time 8 to 10 minutes

Equipment A list of types of learners written on an overhead transparency or flip-chart sheet in advance of the session
An extra name tag for each person

Process *NOTE:* This activity should be preceded by a brief icebreaker.

The trainer gives each participant an extra name tag and posts the following information on an overhead transparency or flip-chart sheet.

Four types of learners come into a training setting. See if you can find yourself among them:

- *An Expert:* Someone with experience and expertise they are willing to share

- *A Vacationer:* Someone there for the "fun" of it, who wants to keep things light

- *A Learner:* An active participator who wants to know who, what, when, where, why, and how

- *A Prisoner:* Someone who doesn't want to be there but has to be for job reasons

The trainer asks participants to decide to which category they belong and to write it on their second name tag, which serves to acknowledge expertise, intellectual curiosity, resistance, and so forth, and lighten the stress level in the class.

Options The trainer can ask everyone to check whether their categories have changed after the afternoon break or at the beginning of the second day of training.

Some trainers may wish to add "judge" as a category.

The trainer may choose to go over each role, reassuring participants that their roles are valued, for example:

- For the Expert: "I assure you, you will have many opportunities to share your good ideas and knowledge with others."

- For the Vacationer: "I assure you, you will have opportunities to meet and mingle and talk with others."

- For the Learner: "You are most welcome, for you are ready and willing to learn, and I and the other participants will do all we can to answer your questions."

- For the Prisoner: "I assure you, we will have breaks, and we will not go over the agreed-on time."

- For the Judge: "I assure you, evaluation forms will be forthcoming."

Worst Day Ever

☑ Icebreaker

☐ Networker

☑ Team Builder

☑ Task Tension

☑ Relationship Tension

☐ Personal Tension

☑ Focus Activity

Objectives   Break the ice
Allow opportunities to build teams
Relieve the tension associated with a topic
Become better acquainted
Provide focus on the topic

Class Length   Ninety minutes or longer

Audience   Any group learning material for which there may be resistance

Group Size   Any number, in subgroups of five to seven

Time   8 to 10 minutes

Equipment   A piece of blank paper for each subgroup
Pens or pencils for participants

Process   *NOTE:* If the group consists of ten or fewer participants, this exercise can be done by everyone in the room; with larger groups, team efforts can result in a wonderfully humorous sharing.

To help participants discuss the stress involved in what they are going to be learning, the trainer begins by asking participants individually, or as teams, to collaborate in building "worst day ever" scenarios. The trainer starts it off with something like, "My alarm didn't go off this morning . . ." and asks everyone to add a phrase until the day is complete, for example: "and then I burned my toast so I didn't have anything to eat . . .," "I tripped over my daughter's bike and cut my shin . . .," "an accident caused the traffic to move so slowly that I was late to work . . .," and so on.

If the group is working in teams, scribes are selected to write down the scenarios as each person in the group adds a sentence. When all groups have finished, all groups are asked to share with everyone else in the room.

The trainer then leads a discussion of all the stresses that build up about learning new information or performing in new ways after a training session.

Option   This activity can be adapted to various training situations by changing the "worst day ever" to the "worst day as a customer service rep" or the "worst day as a manager or customer."

Write a Commercial

Objectives Break the ice
Become better acquainted
Provide focus on the topic

Class Length One day or longer

Audience Any

Group Size Any number, in pairs or in subgroups of five to seven

Time 15 to 20 minutes

Equipment One copy of the Writing a Commercial Assignment for each person
Blank 8½" x 11" paper for each participant
A pen or pencil for each participant

Process The trainer has the group form into pairs or small subgroups and spend a bit of time getting acquainted (if necessary), gives copies of the writing assignment, blank paper, and a pen or pencil to each person, then gives everyone time to work on their commercials. Afterward, everyone shares what they have written with the whole group or the smaller groups.

Option   The entire class could be considered the "client," in which case the assignment would be to interview the instructor, review course materials, and so on, then write the commercials either individually or as a team.

Writing a Commercial Assignment

Assignment: Pretend that you are employed by an advertising agency that has just taken on a new client (your partner). The client wants the agency to write a 30-second radio commercial that promotes his or her good points.

Using the rules of good advertising copy, the client's name must be used six times.

Eight strong points should be made, "selling" the client's good qualities.

You might approach this assignment as: "Here are some reasons you should hire this person" or "Here are some reasons you would like to have this person for a friend."

After writing the commercial for your partner, time it and make it as close to thirty seconds as you can.

About the Authors

☑ Icebreaker

☑ Networker

☑ Team Builder

☑ Task Tension

☑ Relationship Tension

☑ Personal Tension

☑ Focus Activity

Bob Pike, CSP, CPAE

Bob Pike has developed and implemented training programs for business, industry, government, and the professions since 1969. He began his career as a representative for Master Education Industries, where he moved up to become senior vice president. His responsibilities included developing an intensive three-week Master Training Academy, which covered all phases of sales training, management development, communications, motivation/platform skills, and business operations.

During his five years as vice president of Personal Dynamics, Inc., that company grew from fewer than four thousand enrollments per year to more than eighty thousand. He pioneered undergraduate and graduate credit on a national basis. As CEO and founder of Creative Training Techniques Press and Creative Training Techniques International, Inc., Bob leads sessions over 150 days per year, covering the topics of leadership, attitudes, motivation, communication, decision making, problem solving, personal and organizational effectiveness, conflict management, team building, and managerial productivity. More than 75,000 trainers have attended the Creative Training Techniques® workshop. As a consultant Bob has worked with such organizations as Pfizer, Upjohn, Caesar's Boardwalk Regency, *Exhibitor Magazine,* Hallmark Cards, Inc., and IBM.

A member of the American Society for Training and Development (ASTD) since 1972, Bob has been active in many capacities. He is currently serving on the Board of Directors for the National Speakers' Association (NSA) and the International Alliance of Learning. He has presented at regional and national ASTD and Training Conferences. In 1991 he was granted the professional designation of Certified Speaking Professional (CSP) by the National Speakers Association (NSA). In 1999 he was inducted into the NSA CPAE (Council of Peers Award of Excellence) Speaker's Hall of Fame. Since 1980, he has been listed in the *Who's Who in the Midwest* and is listed in the current edition of *Who's Who in Finance and Industry*. Over the years, Bob has contributed to *TRAINING* magazine, *The Personnel Administrator,* and *The Self-Development Journal*. He is editor of the *Creative Training Techniques Newsletter* and is author of *The Creative Training Techniques Handbook, Developing, Marketing and Promoting Successful Seminars and Workshops,* and *Improving Managerial Productivity.*

Lynn Solem (1934–1999)

Since December of 1986, Lynn has delivered over 6,000 hours of Creative Training Techniques.® She has delivered specialty aspects of Creative Training Techniques for Lakewood Publications' Best of America and Total Trainer Conferences. Lynn has created and delivered seminars and workshops on such topics as sales skills, interpersonal communications, team building, leadership skills, communication styles, problem solving, and managing service as a corporate asset.

Formerly the executive vice president and chief executive officer at Personal Dynamics, Inc., she was responsible for developing and marketing materials used in seminars, training, and workshop settings. Lynn has received many national awards, been selected as "Outstanding Young Woman of America," and been inducted into the United Nations Hall of Fame.

Lynn's consulting clients have included: General Dynamics, EDS, MCI Pacific and Midwest Divisions, the U.S. Postal Service, IBM, Pennsylvania Power and Light, the U.S. Bureau of Patents, the Houston Independent School District, the National School Board Association, the Federal Bureau of Prisons, Southwestern Bell Telephone, and Consolidated Edison.

More great resources from Jossey-Bass/Pfeiffer!

End your sessions with a BANG!

Lynn Solem
& Bob Pike

50 Creative Training Closers

They'll forget you as soon as you walk out the door—unless you make your training memorable. This essential resource is your way to make your mark. Fifty ways to close your training sessions and presentations so they won't forget you—or your training.

Many trainers start training sessions memorably with a rousing icebreaker, or with a spirited overview of what's to follow. But you're probably letting the ends slip through your fingers. Some trainers conclude training sessions by looking at their watches and saying, "Oh, time's up! Goodbye!" By trailing off with a whisper, you're missing an opportunity to reinforce your training. You're helping your participants to forget everything you've taught them. Stop this brain drain by ending with a bang! This invaluable book is packed with practical closers.

You get activities great for:

- *Reviewing* material
- *Celebrating* success
- *Motivating* participants . . . and more!

Solem and Pike show you all the essentials, and preparation is quick and easy. So little time to invest for such a HUGE payoff! This book is training dynamite—make it your secret weapon today.

paperback / 96 pages

50 Creative Training Closers
Item #F439

Bob Pike &
Dave Arch

Dealing with Difficult Participants

127 Practical Strategies for Minimizing Resistance and Maximizing Results in Your Presentations

Everyone knows them . . . but almost no one knows how to deal with them. Difficult participants. The "latecomer." The "know-it-all." The "confused." What do you do? Train-the-trainer master Bob Pike and magician/trainer Dave Arch have the answers.

Learn to deal with types such as:

- The Preoccupied
- The Socializer
- The Introvert
- The Bored
- The Domineering
- The Unqualified
- The Skeptic
- The Sleeper . . . and others!

Don't let difficult participants get the best of you. You can't afford not to pick up this engaging book. Maximize the learning potential in all your presentations with *Dealing With Difficult Participants*!

paperback / 150 pages

Dealing with Difficult Participants
Item #F244

To order, please contact your local bookstore, call us toll-free at 1-800-274-4434, or visit us on the Web at www.pfeiffer.com.

13 Questions to Ask *Before* You Bring Anyone In-House

An in-house program is an investment. You want to ensure high return. Here are 13 questions to ask before you ask anyone to train your trainers (or train anyone else!).

1. What kind of measurable results have other clients had from your training?
2. How much experience does this company have in training trainers?
3. Is this 100 percent of what the company does or just part of what it does?
4. How experienced are the trainers who will work with our people?
5. How experienced are your trainers in maximizing training transfer to the job?
6. Is the program tailored to my needs, or is it the same content as the public program?
7. Why is an in-house program to our advantage?
8. Is team-building a by-product of the seminar?
9. Is there immediate application of new skills during the training session?
10. What kinds of resource and reference materials do we get?
11. What type of pre-course preparation or post-course follow-up do you do?
12. How are our participants recognized for their achievements?
13. Will you teach my trainers how to get participant buy-in, even from the difficult participant?

Advantages of a Customized, In-House Program with Creative Training Techniques™ International, Inc.

Customized in-house programs provide your organization with training tailored to your specific needs. Our unique participant-centered teaching style is a revolutionary new training approach that is far more effective than traditional lecture-based training. This training approach has been adapted by a wide range of industries including healthcare, finance, communications, government, and non-profit agencies. Our clients include American Express, AT&T, Hewlett-Packard, 3M, U.S. Healthcare, and Tonka Corporation. We are eager to learn about your training needs and discuss how we can provide solutions. Please give us a call so we can help your company create a more vital and effective workforce.

Creative Training Techniques
International, Inc.

1-800-383-9210
www.cttbobpike.com

Creative Training Techniques International, Inc. • 7620 W. 78th St., Mpls., MN 55439 • 612-829-1954 • Fax 612-829-0260

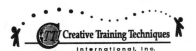
6451